TRANSFORMING PRACTICES

Finding Joy and Satisfaction in the Legal Life

TENTH ANNIVERSARY EDITION

BY STEVEN KEEVA

AMERICAN BAR ASSOCIATION
Defending Liberty
Pursuing Justice

Transforming Practices

This American Bar Association edition is an unabridged republication of *Transforming Practices: Finding Joy and Satisfaction in the Legal Life*, originally published by Contemporary Books, a division of the McGraw-Hill Companies, in 1999.

Printed in the United States of America

12 11 10 09 08 5 4 3 2 1

Library of Congress Cataloging-in-Publication Data

Keeva, Steven.
  Transforming practices : finding joy and satisfaction in the legal life / Steven Keeva.
      p. cm.
  Includes bibliographical references and index.
  ISBN-13: 978-1-60442-729-5 (alk. paper)
  ISBN-10: 1-60442-729-9 (alk. paper)
  1. Practice of law—Moral and ethical aspects. 2. Lawyers. 3. Legal ethics. I. Title.
  K123.K44 2009
  340.023—dc22

                                                                    2009044906

Discounts are available for books ordered in bulk. Special consideration is given to state bars, CLE programs, and other bar-related organizations. Inquire at Book Publishing, ABA Publishing, American Bar Association, 321 North Clark Street, Chicago, Illinois 60654-7598. www.ababooks.org

For Jan, Aidan, and Anna Rose

Praise for Transforming Practices

"Steve Keeva was among the first to recognize that the pervasive unhappiness throughout so much of the legal profession was not the product of a problem with the profession itself. Rather, it was due, in large measure, to the limited vision so many lawyers shared of *how* to practice law, a vision forged first in law school and reinforced in practice. So Steve traveled the country and spoke with many, many extraordinary individuals who had transformed their own practices in ways that comported with their core, humanistic values. And then he wrote this wonderful book that told their stories. His work continues to inspire increasing numbers of incredible lawyers and law professors seeking to make the practice of law more humane, more healing, more fulfilling, both for themselves and for their clients. I am a grateful beneficiary of his wisdom and insights."

Marjorie A. Silver
Professor of Law, Touro Law Center, Central Islip, N.Y., and editor of
and contributing author to The Affective Assistance of Counsel:
Practicing Law as a Healing Profession

"The inspirational Steve Keeva, through this book and his other writings, made it possible and legitimate for me to work as a professional offering programs bringing contemplative practices to lawyers. May this new edition continue to imbue the legal profession with balance!"

Douglas Chermak
Law Program Director, Center for Contemplative Mind in Society

"Steven Keeva's book is the pioneering effort to examine what should be every lawyer's ultimate goal—to find joy in the practice of law! Every member of the bar should have a copy of this book so that when you get off-track, Steven can remind you of what's really important in life."

Ronald M. Martin
Of Counsel, Holland & Hart

"I met Steve when I was in an Innovative Lawyers Group with Stu Webb and others in the mid-90s. Steve's dedication to helping lawyers transform as their practices transform has impacted me in the following ways:

1. Finding my 'core' gave me the strength to give up all court and adversarial work over a decade ago. By declaring myself as a peacemaker, my skills and practice thrived beyond all expectations;

2. I use the possibility of transformation in all my teaching and training. It not only helps make material more relevant and interesting—it gives students and practitioners a real model for which to strive;

3. I use life values as a platform for congruently marketing my practice and have incorporated focus on values as a source for my writing on both skills and practice building—and writing guides for other professionals."

Forrest S. Mosten
Mediator and Collaborative Attorney

"As a former paralegal/legal secretary who has worked for hundreds of attorneys, I've seen too much how the pains of the legal profession today impact not just lawyers but also their spouses, children, staff, and everyone else in our society.

Thanks to Steven Keeva's reporting, we now know so much more about the heart and soul of law, and how the best practice of law combines sharp legal thinking with compassion, creativity, integrity, laughter, and time to enjoy life. We also have had the benefit of his many years of helping those with a longing to bring out the best in the profession to find each other.

So much has happened since *Transforming Practices* first came out. Though Steven can't report on all the benefits of all the connections he's helped make, there's no better book in which to ground the transformation of law.

Actually, *Transforming Practices* is the best book I've seen anywhere about how to restore the soul of any profession or any worker. Trends may come, statistics may change, but the juicy stories and simple instructions in this book will endure."

Pat McHenry Sullivan
Co-founder, Spirit and Work Resource Center
Author, Work with Meaning, Work with Joy

"The health of our profession depends on every lawyer taking the occasional respite to assess his or her emotional and spiritual well-being. In *Transforming Practices*, Steven Keeva provides an oasis where our profession can reflect on where it has been and where it wants to go. This inspiring, instructive, and utterly readable book helps the reader achieve a life that is both richer and more fulfilling."

Robert Hirshon
Former President, The American Bar Association

"*Transforming Practices* should be required reading in law school so that lawyers not only practice more successfully in the years ahead, but, perhaps more importantly, don't end up throwing away years of their lives before they decide it's finally time to start living. I highly recommend this well-written and scholarly book for every member of the legal profession."

Vincent Bugliosi
Attorney and Author of Helter Skelter *and other bestsellers*

"A deeply inspired and inspiring book. Keeva offers a compelling account of what lawyers need to do, individually and collectively, to bring greater fulfillment to their legal practice. By exploring strategies for integrating personal and professional values, this book brings new insights to long-standing problems. It reminds us of our deepest values and the need to make them central in our working lives."

Deborah L. Rhode
McFarland Professor of Law and Director of the
Stanford Center of the Legal Profession

"Steven Keeva's book makes three great contributions to lawyers and the profession. First, with easily understood language, he invites lawyers to look inward and to integrate their inner and outer lives. He provides practical, grounded exercises for exploring the inner life. Second, he tells striking stories of lawyers, firms, and law schools which are building spiritual practice into their activities. Third, he calls on concerned members of the legal community to launch a new spiritual conversation which could transform legal institutions and benefit the country."

Charles Halpern
Former President, Nathan Cummings Foundation Founding Dean,
City University of New York School of Law

"*Transforming Practices* sends its message loud and clear: you are not alone in your disappointment with today's prevailing law practice model, nor are you powerless to change things for the better. The stories in this book will inspire you to change your attitude toward the law, your approach to practice, and ultimately, your profession."

Deborah Arron
Author of What Can You Do with a Law Degree?
and Running from the Law: Why Good Lawyers
Are Getting Out of the Legal Profession

"A terrific book, *Transforming Practices* is a concisely yet profoundly written *Spiritual Exercises* for the practice of law in America today . . . *Transforming Practices* is more than worth every lawyer's time."

Lawrence Joseph
Author of Lawyerland

"Good lawyers are healers and problem solvers. They know how to listen to a client, understand the client's problem or opportunity, and serve as a counselor rather than a gladiator. Sometimes the best lawyers practice psychiatry without a license. Steven Keeva's book will help lawyers fulfill the profession's highest ideals."

Newton N. Minow
Senior Counsel, Sidley & Austin
Former Chair, Federal Communication Commission
Former Chair, National Public Radio

"Every lawyer in America will want to read Steve Keeva's new book, *Transforming Practices*. Why? Because you will find in it answers to the silent questions that haunt your nights. Because you will glimpse new possibilities. Because it will fill you with hope . . . for a renewed legal profession . . . for the vital work of lawyers . . . and for your own rich place in this world."

Merrilyn Astin Tarlton
President, Astin Tarlton Consulting

"If *Transforming Practices* makes one thing clear, it is this: the seeds of meaning and satisfaction can be found within the life of the productive lawyer, but you have to know where—and how—to look. Steven Keeva shows you a way that is both practical and attainable. I wish such a book existed when I was practicing law, and it will surely be on the required reading list of my in-house legal staff."

David A. Grant
Former President, Fox Television Studios

CONTENTS

FOREWORD

It was 1999. I had lost my wife, I lost my job, even my cat had died, but I was not alone. I was not sure what the future held, but I knew that the past was over. And that I was "done" with practicing law. But I knew that I was not alone. I learned this at the conference of the International Alliance of Holistic Lawyers. What lawyers?! Holistic lawyers.

That year's conference was filled with other attorneys who had at some point lost their way in the law. Perhaps I was not such a freak or loser after all. And it was filled with attorneys marking a path for new ways to practice law. They were working in Collaborative Law, Therapeutic Jurisprudence, Restorative Justice, Humanizing Legal Education. They were law school faculty and administrators, yoga instructors, mediators, shamans, and litigators.

The IAHL had been formed to bring together attorneys who had lost their passion, lost their connection, lost their souls to the law ... and had found their way back. And in the middle of this group of holistic lawyers who had found their way back to their hearts and their souls and to the possibility of joy and satisfaction in the legal life, I met the man who was telling our stories to the world.

Steven Keeva is not a man who dominates a room or a conversation with his grand statements, gestures, or even huge ideas or pronouncements. He is a man who stands out for his heart, for his genuine compassion. Steve is not to be found in a crowded room at the center of a cluster of dedicated listeners. Rather, you find Steve in a room by looking for the place where people patiently stand waiting for a chance to speak to the man. For Steve is, above all else, a genuine, caring listener. He is also an excellent teller of others' tales.

This book, *Transforming Practices*, had just been published. I had not yet read the book. I was not even aware of it at that time. However, most of the other lawyers in the room were already aware of it. Indeed, several of them were featured in it. Why? Why did this book cause such a stir among so many attorneys?

Much of what this book is about is restoring the practice of law to a proper priority in a person's life: integrating it into a full rich life, rather than allowing it to displace family, friends, and ideals. It shows, with the vivid stories of those highlighted and the wise insights and valuable exercises it presents, that each of us does have a choice in how we practice law. If it is done without losing one's self, both the practitioner and the world can benefit greatly.

It's been 10 years since that conference. And in June of this year, 2009, I had the honor of standing before the 17th annual conference of the IAHL as its president. In that role, it pleased me deeply to be able to present to Steve Keeva the IAHL's first Transforming Practices Award. We all listened with knowing smiles as those gathered in the room and by videotape from across the country shared stories of the impact Steve Keeva's book had had on our practices and our lives. We all knew we were not alone.

Thank you, Steve. It's a joy knowing you and a privilege to be able to welcome your book back to the shelves for a new wave of lawyers looking to find their own way—their own joy and satisfaction—in the legal life.

CARL MICHAEL ROSSI, MA, JD, LPC
President, 2008–2010
International Alliance of Holistic Lawyers

PREFACE

SOME TIME AGO, IN AN ESSAY ENTITLED "SEEING NATURE WHOLE," the novelist John Fowles made an observation that changed the way I look at the natural world. His point was simple, but profound: beneath the paved landscapes in which we live, the earth remains alive, its generative potential unbroken. To the extent that we think of it at all, Fowles wrote, we tend to assume the land is dead, smothered by the man-made overlay.

This book is partly about ways in which the demands of legal life can function like cement and asphalt to obliterate from view what lies below, in the hearts and minds of lawyers.

I believe there is abundant life beneath the professional overlay, but that the legal culture sits carelessly upon it, making it too great a challenge for shoots of feeling and awareness to find the light. Some lawyers have always been able to see through the elaborate veneer: others are coming around now, searching for the right conditions in which to let their inner selves blossom. This book represents an attempt to help establish those conditions in the lives of lawyers so that a transformation of the legal landscape can begin to come about.

In nearly a decade of legal journalism, I've written about criminal, constitutional, environmental, international, entertainment, military, and other types of law. But what I've enjoyed most is writing about lawyers, as people. I find it gratifying to talk to them, to be honored with their confidences.

I have had countless conversations about the influences that shaped lawyers' professional lives, many of them about law school. Of those, a particular story stands out in my mind, one offered by a Colorado lawyer who recalled being taken aback when, just after finishing his legal education, he ran into an old friend. After they chatted a while, the friend looked at him, his face filled with bewilderment and concern. "What, exactly, did they *do* to you in there to make you come out this way?" he asked.

In the first year, he replied, they told him to erase everything he thought he knew. Then, in the second year, they showed him how he could advocate for any position, regardless of what he thought or felt about it. By the third year, they had him thinking like a lawyer, job done.

I offer this story here because of the light I think it sheds on what I hope to accomplish in this book. I believe *Transforming Practices* inverts the Colorado lawyer's description of what law school does to you. Instead of progressively narrowing your field of vision—year by year by year— each of the book's three main parts opens into something larger, representing an expansion of possibilities and a rebirth of hope.

If the goal of law school is to teach you to think like a lawyer, the goal of this book is to enhance the experience of *being* a lawyer by reminding you of how you can, and why you should, cultivate your innate ability to think, feel, and *be* exactly what you are—a human being.

Steven Keeva

ACKNOWLEDGMENTS

AT THE VERY BEGINNING OF THIS PROJECT, my wife made me promise to keep a running list of people whose help made it all possible. Alas, her concern was justified. Having been only intermittently vigilant in the task she proposed, I now see that I have done exactly what she hoped to help me avoid. And so, if the list that follows is incomplete, I have only myself to blame.

Many of the people I wish to thank can be acknowledged in the traditional way, by name, but some cannot. And yet, these unnamed contributors have been among the most helpful of all. These are the innumerable lawyers to whom I've spoken over the years without whose experience and observations this book could not have been written. Some of them appear in the following pages with their names changed in respect for their privacy. A few—*very* few—have been conflated into composites that exemplify important points. To all of these lawyers, wherever they may be, I am deeply grateful.

I thank Gary Hengstler for believing in this work, and for demonstrating that belief again and again; Danielle Egan-Miller of Contemporary

Books for her early excitement and enthusiastic support throughout; Caroline Carney of Bookdeals, Inc., for her expertise and endless encouragement; Anne Basye for her indispensable editorial help; Robert Yates for his generosity and support during these many years; my colleagues at the *ABA Journal* for their patience and forbearance during the long months when my mind was so often otherwise engaged; and the *ABA Journal* Board of Editors, particularly Bill Haltom for his leadership and vision.

Other people who have, alone and in the aggregate, made an incalculable contribution to this book include Rob Lehman and Paul Ginter of the Fetzer Institute for their kind support, and for paving the way to something new and better; Michael Gergely; Jon Kabat-Zinn, Lawrence Horwitz, and Ferris Urbanowski of the Center for Mindfulness in Medicine, Health Care, and Society; David Hall of Northeastern University; John Hamilton; Hon. Jon Levy; Hon. William Schma; Mihaly Csikszentmihalyi; David Link; David Soucy; Milner Ball; Cheryl Conner; Tom Porter; John McShane; Stephen Chakwin; Judi Neal; Irwin Stolz; Terry Stein, M.D.; Carroll Straus; M. Beth Krugler; Bonnie Sashin; Merrilyn Astin Tarlton; Hons. Dorothy and James Nelson; Mirabai Bush; Donna Spilis; Helen Desmond McDonald; and William van Zyverden.

On a more personal level, thanks are due—and always have been due—to the friends and family who sustain me in every way, beginning with my wife, Jan, to whom simply saying thanks feels pretty feeble after all she did to make this book possible. Also, my grandparents, Herman "Peep" and Sadie Hershkowitz; my sisters, Sue Keeva and Debbie Kiva; Judy (my mom) and Max Houston; Danny Keeva; the Schneiderman clan; Bob and Lois Ellenstein; Michael Skovron; Lawrence Greenstein; Scooter; David Grant; John Knickelbine; Kate and Paul Russell; Michael and Jane Sparks; our Evanston friends (you know who you are) for logistical and moral support; Jon Jefferson; Mark Hansen; Teri Leichenger; Rhonda Rosen; Julia Zaetta; David Ellenstein and Denise Young; Peter Ellenstein; Linda Warren; and, of course, Keva Rosenfeld—for the ever-loving Shmaig of it. Finally, my love and heartfelt thanks to Kerry Murphy, whose memory is a continual inspiration.

ACKNOWLEDGMENTS FOR THE TENTH ANNIVERSARY EDITION

In addition to the wonderful people who I thanked in the first edition, I am also grateful to all the people who have supported me in the last ten years and those who have been the unrelenting force behind this new edition: carl Michael rossi, Kim Wright, Michael Matthews, Kevin E. Houchin, Erin Nevius, Sheila Webber, Ray Nimrod, the members of the IAHL, and once again, my friend, John McShane. If I have forgotten to mention anyone, please forgive me—ten years is a long time.

INTRODUCTION

The way we spend our days is the way we spend our lives.
—Annie Dillard

Life does not seem to be impressed by our arguments
that we can ignore our deeper desires simply because
we happen to be earning a living at the time.
—David Whyte
The Heart Aroused

WHEN I TOLD PEOPLE THAT I WAS writing a book about spirituality and the practice of law, they overwhelmingly reacted with the same question: "Isn't that an oxymoron?" The problem, it turned out, was with the word *spirituality*. It has a Rorschach quality to it. We see in it what our experience leads us to see, and often we remain unaware of other possibilities. I've found that people most often hear it as a synonym for religion or a cover for so-called New Age thought and lifestyles.

For the purposes of this book, both reactions miss the mark. I believe that our spirituality is that inner part of us where we are sensitive to the deepest, most nuanced levels of meaning in our lives. It is also the part that is capable of apprehending the sacred in the everyday. In *The Music of Silence*, David Steindl-Rast defines spirituality this way:

> Sometimes people get the mistaken notion that spirituality is a sepa-
> rate department of life, the penthouse of our existence. But rightly
> understood, it is a vital awareness that pervades all realms of our being.
> Someone will say, "I come alive when I listen to music," or "I come to
> life when I garden," or "I come alive when I play golf." Wherever we
> come alive, that is the area in which we are spiritual. . . . To be vital,
> awake, aware, in all areas of our lives, is the task that is never accom-
> plished, but it remains the goal.

Sadly, the inner life is often left underdeveloped in people who live hurriedly, under the weight of constant deadlines and pressures. This lack of development is particularly unfortunate among lawyers because so many can recall—often with a twinge of sadness for that which has not come to pass—the spiritual impulses that brought them to the law in the first place.

Spiritual impulses? Here's what I mean: To the extent that you enter it as a calling, the practice of law is about hunger—the hunger for reso-lution; for healing the lives of individuals, organizations, and communi-ties; for enabling society to function harmoniously and productively; and ultimately, for justice. Spirituality may not always be easy to define, but the concept is certainly embodied in these yearnings, as it is in any quest to deepen your understanding of what it means to live a good and meaningful life. When lawyers express in words and actions that they feel caught between a professional role and who they really are, they are describing a personal spiritual crisis—a crisis that is much talked about in law schools and law firms, albeit in somewhat different terms.

In society today, evidence of a great search for meaning is every-where—in the words of popular songs, in the pages of *The New York Times* and other prominent newspapers and magazines, in movies and in spiritually oriented books, whose sales increased 800 percent between 1993 and 1998 and have continued to rise since. It isn't a matter of high or low culture; this yearning crosses barriers of style and education, race and ethnicity. People simply are looking for new ways of knowing and being.

Lawyers, too, yearn for meaning, even though the traditional legal culture has neither acknowledged the importance of the inner life to its members, nor invited the possibility that it is in the spiritual domain—above and beyond the ethical guidelines that govern professional behavior—that a deeper flowering of lawyers' humanity and an attendant leap in satisfaction might be realized. Neglecting the connection has contributed significantly to the malaise that now grips a significant and expanding segment of the profession.

To a lawyer, a law student, or someone considering applying to law school, the cultivation of a deeper and more vibrant inner life can promise a great deal, all of it compelling, much of it eminently practical. It can bring meaning and excitement to your practice; it can help you relate better with clients, and allow you to handle the pressures and vicissitudes of law practice with equanimity; it can make you a better, clearer, more focused and balanced lawyer, and in so doing enhance your value and relevance to the legal profession. Finally, attention to the spiritual, or inner, dimension can help you deepen or reclaim a sense of purpose in your work and make clearer how the path you're on—the legal path—can enhance and deepen your experience of life.

This book examines the spiritual crisis in the legal profession and shows how lawyers are taking the first tentative steps to address it. It examines seven kinds of spiritually oriented law practices in chapters that highlight approaches, techniques, and mind-sets that can be truly transforming, in the sense of fundamentally changing the experience of practicing law. I hope that its contents will help you achieve balance in your life; become more aware of the options that each moment offers, even in the midst of pressures and demands; realize the extraordinary opportunities the profession provides for personal growth; and find a satisfying vision for your future in the law.

In a 1972 speech at Harvard Law School, the poet Archibald MacLeish, himself a graduate of that institution, exhorted lawyers not to forget that they are, above all, members of the human family. He said, "We have to treat others as a part of who we are, rather than as a 'them' with whom we are in constant competition." That notion—one that is common to every great spiritual tradition—has profound implications for our society, the legal profession, and individual lawyers. It isn't always easy, in the context of a law practice, to do what MacLeish insists must be done, but it certainly is possible. There have always been lawyers who have managed to do it, and they are the ones who inspire others to make our common humanity their touchstone and beacon. In today's legal climate, there may be fewer such lawyers around, but they are out there, and their ideas and experiences—as well as the pleasure they take in their work—are worthy of our devoted attention.

PART ONE

A MAP OF
THE WORLD

Only those who are lost will find
the promised land.

—*Abraham Joshua Heschel*

CHAPTER ONE

TERRA COGNITA

An unfulfilled vocation drains the color
from a man's entire existence.
—*Honoré de Balzac*

IF YOU WERE TO SURVEY THE LAWYERS you know to find out what led them to the law, you would probably come across reasons as diverse as the people you asked. Some would acknowledge enticements of prestige and respect; others, the intellectual challenge, power, or money. Some—those willing to admit it—would likely say they were not enticed at all; they simply succumbed to family pressures or to the popular notion that law practice provides a better home than most careers for bright people who aren't quite sure what they want to do with their lives. Still, one reason might be somewhat more common than the rest: the desire to help people solve their problems. The truth is that for those who've sought an ennobling sense of mission in their work, the law has long held out the chance of finding it—by solving people's problems in the name of social harmony and justice.

Ironically, a growing number of legal professionals, though dedicated and skilled at solving other people's problems, are today facing a problem of their own. Too many have followed the unwritten rules, taken the right courses and made the right contacts along the way, only to find themselves nowhere near the sense of fulfillment they had anticipated. There is a hole at the center of their professional lives.

The legal profession, like all other cultures, functions a bit like a huge campfire around which people tell stories deep into the night. Whether the stories are humorous, outrageous, poignant, or distressing, together they capture the tone and texture of what it feels like to practice law today. Increasingly, they speak of growing discomfort in the way lives are being affected by perceived obligations and questionable tactics that have changed the face of the profession. "I got into this because I thought I could help make the world a better place," says one litigator, "but I'm not helping anyone. There's no human connection. All I'm doing is helping the stream of commerce."

Sadly, the most compelling story today is told not in words, but in the hauntingly articulate language of illness and dysfunction. Dissatisfaction wears many faces—these days, far too many—and those faces are looking increasingly desperate.

At the law school level, school-supplied psychologists are seeing a disturbingly high incidence of students who suffer from debilitating levels of stress, accompanied by feelings of alienation and low self-esteem, along with such physical ailments as insomnia and digestive problems. Many report chronic fear of humiliation and the feeling that it isn't safe to talk about anything personal or "real" with classmates.

In the world of law practice, it only gets worse. Studies show that one of every four lawyers suffers from psychological distress of some kind. The most common complaints include feelings of inadequacy and inferiority in relationships, as well as anxiety, social alienation, and isolation.

A California study showed a majority of lawyers saying that if they had the chance, they would not become lawyers again, and well over half said they would not recommend law as a career to their own children.

The figures on substance abuse are no less alarming. While 15 to 18 percent of the nation's lawyers abuse alcohol or drugs, the number in the population at large is 10 percent. According to some statewide studies, substance abuse is a factor in up to 75 percent of disciplinary complaints involving lawyers.

Perhaps the most troubling findings, however, come from a Johns Hopkins University study that looked at the incidence of depression among members of 105 different occupations. Lawyers topped the list. Depression can be a precursor to physical illness and—at its worst—suicide, so its underlying causes are worth exploring. One explanation comes from the work of Victor Frankl, a pathbreaking psychiatrist and author of *Man's Search for Meaning*.

After spending three years in Nazi concentration camps, Frankl, a Viennese Jew, emerged with one overriding question: What was it that made some prisoners give in to despair and sometimes suicide while others not only survived but even found moments of joy amid the suffering? He found that those who could find meaning in their agony were the ones who survived or even thrived in spite of the inhumanity of their surroundings. For Frankl, the search for meaning in life is *the* primary human motivation.

Clearly, there is no comparison to be made between the contemporary legal profession and Nazi death camps, nor is any intended. But the lesson regarding the vital role of a personal sense of meaning may be instructive, for too many lawyers have lost this sense in their careers.

It is essential to be clear about where people find meaning in their lives. No matter how times change, the list of enduring sources remains essentially the same:

- relationships
- giving back to society
- creating something that endures
- possessing a sense of divinity, holiness, or awe
- being in love
- working productively
- suffering

What these sources of meaning have in common is that they all, to varying degrees, suggest a coming together of the outer world and the inner life, each being enriched to the extent that a deep inner engagement is brought to the experience. Relationships, for example, are most meaningful when you bring your deepest feelings and capacity for openness to them. So, too, for contributing to society, where the truest and most satisfying experience of giving is always that which is a true expression of one's inner self. Suffering over a painful event is a particularly good example of how the inner and outer selves come together to create meaning. The same external event will have a different meaning for everyone who experiences it, depending at least partly on the depth and vitality of an individual's inner life.

LAW SCHOOL: A MAP WITHOUT MEANING

We all carry maps in our minds, put there by the experiences and influences that shape us and show us where we stand in the world. They chart the topography of meaning in our lives. At first, their features are supplied by family, friends, teachers, and the larger society, whose collective influences combine with our own gifts and perceptions to create a unique understanding of how to cope with life's pitfalls while seeking its pleasures. These inner maps describe the territories of our feelings and beliefs, our passions and convictions. In our early lives and through our teens, they tend to be dynamic, evolving as we intuit the basic laws of relationships and the nature of friendship, cooperation, and reciprocity, and come to recognize the variety of feelings that accompany different kinds of human connections.

For many—perhaps most—who choose the legal path, this changes in law school. Few would deny that those three years amount to a profoundly formative, indeed a *trans*formative, experience, one that reconfigures students' inner maps. In the minds of the great pioneers of legal education, that was exactly what it meant to do.

For the likes of Christopher Columbus Langdell and Oliver Wendell Holmes, law was a science consisting of principles and doctrines applied, as Langdell put it, "to the very-tangled skein of human affairs." The tool Holmes recommended to students was "cynical acid," used to burn away the language of right and wrong and thereby reveal the law as it *really* is. This, Holmes believed, would put the law on a truly scientific footing.

These innovators were concerned that the law be seen as a legitimate discipline, apart from, say, political science or theology. It had to be self-contained, separate from the larger context of human activity. The problem was that for all the good that came of their work—and the analytical tools they provided are clearly essential—one message was clear: Not only are morality and spirituality *not* fundamental to the enterprise, they are at best marginal and at worst antithetical to the lawyer's goals. In *The Path of the Law*, Holmes put it this way: "I often wonder if it would not be a gain if every word of moral significance could be banished from the law altogether."

The problem with such notions, relative to the dilemma facing so many lawyers today, is this: while Holmes, his colleagues, and their progeny may have produced a system unexcelled in its ability to train the mind to produce airtight, unassailable legal arguments, they also managed to marginalize most of human experience. If you imagine a Venn diagram in which two circles overlap, one containing the seven sources of meaning listed earlier and the other representing the law school experience, the only obvious point of commonality—the source of meaning almost certain to be satisfied in law school—is "working productively." Although "giving back to society" and "creating something that endures" are possibilities, they are rarely granted the same status as intellectual prowess or finding a job at a prestigious law firm. Such an imagined diagram offers a troubling reminder of the limited scope of meaning in law school.

The legacy of such a system is clear today when lawyers complain, as they so often do, about feeling cut off from others and from those parts of themselves that appear to be irrelevant in a profession that exalts above all else the twin "virtues" of laserlike intelligence and winning— regardless of what that may mean on a human level.

Such gifts as emotional intelligence, compassion, and warmth have little if any standing in the current legal culture. And in a legal academy that extols the economic analysis of legal outcomes while giving almost no consideration to the law's—and law practice's—psychological and emotional effects, students fall under the spell of a legal map that is at odds, in both its narrowness and its lack of mystery and feeling, with life as they lived it prior to law school. In no time flat, intellectual rigor has become their true north, and a mountain range of reason has replaced their old landscapes of feelings, convictions, and beliefs.

In the law today, you run the risk—first in law school, then in practice—of overlooking the central fact of human life that makes laws necessary in the first place—*that we are formed by and exist in a web of relationships.* Our laws are *about* our relationships; they affirm them by clarifying and enforcing the rights and responsibilities that we, as a society, believe they should entail; and they help us deal with them when they founder or fall apart. It is only in its relationship to the *relational* nature of human beings that the law makes any sense. Yet we sometimes make the law *about* relationships more important than the relationships themselves, allowing doctrine to eclipse humanity. You see it every day in law school—where deepening one's humanity is hardly the point—and by the time you're in practice, it has taken hold in your consciousness. The transformation is complete. But you pay a high price, because at bottom the law and lawyers are fundamentally about the *we*-ness of life, and in turning your back on that fact, you cut yourself off from not only personal, but also professional, fulfillment. You also find yourself at the receiving end of jokes and barbs flung about by opportunistic politicians who reason, probably correctly, that you can't go wrong by slinging mud at lawyers.

All but the strongest and most self-assured leave law school with their maps altered. Granted, there is a certain comfort that comes from having internalized a reality that is ostensibly so comprehensive, one that offers an answer for, or at least a methodology for addressing, any problem that might arise. But for all its seeming inclusiveness, the law school map represents such a small part of human experience that, if taken seriously, it threatens to cut you off from your natural instinct to connect with other people.

Derek Haskew, a public-interest lawyer on the Navajo reservation in southeast Utah, is occasionally shocked by the insidiousness of law school's lessons, even though he considers himself sensitive to the effects that legal education had on his worldview.

He recalls a recent conversation with his father, in which the older man wanted his help. He was going through a divorce, and he explained that his wife was very needy, very dependent on him. He asked his son if he thought he should take care of her or let her handle things herself. Haskew recalls the exact words that came out of his mouth in response: "I said, 'The risk was foreseeable, and you assumed the risk. So there is no remedy.' And he said to me, 'You know, Derek, you used to be such a nice guy.'"

THE LAW FIRM MAP: WIN AT ANY COST

At one time, law practice functioned as a corrective for the version of reality that law students were invited to accept as sufficient and true. Back then, the practice could be counted on to introduce the new lawyer to the unpredictably human elements that a mind gorged on theory and precedent could not yet know. The reality often came with a jolt, but lawyers had time to talk to one another, and the neophyte could count on some guidance. By simply walking a new hire to the courthouse and introducing him to the clerk and a judge or two, or by offering tips on the care and feeding of especially difficult clients, a senior attorney could humanize the practice for the younger lawyer and remind him that his presence mattered.

Today it is different. Too often, the law school map gives way to a professional version whose lands are riddled with booby traps. Everyone is a potential adversary. Trust is a mirage on the horizon. Where once seasoned mentors oversaw your need for significance and a sense of belonging early in your career, now they rarely have the time to provide any succor at all, or even to simply describe the dangers that lie in wait. Brutal competition, disloyalty, staggeringly long work hours—these are the features that fill the gaps in the new associate's already inadequate map of the world, and unless a moderating version of reality intercedes, the sounds and stresses of battle will often seep into your dreams.

Beginning in law school and continuing into the practice, the message comes across loud and clear: What really matters is *winning* (never mind that the two lawyers who have arguably had the strongest impact on our culture—Clarence Darrow and the fictional Atticus Finch—lost their most famous cases). From this primary message flows a number of secondary directives: never admit ignorance; never let your weakness show (better yet, to be sure that doesn't happen, don't even acknowledge it to yourself); develop a mask that suggests certainty, aggressiveness, strength (which, more than likely, you will come to confuse with your real face); kill or be killed.

Many lawyers come to see this pose as a sign of individuality, but really it is not, as psychologist-lawyer Benjamin Sells points out in *The Soul of the Law*. Because it allows for no quirkiness or eccentricity, it is actually "conformity masquerading as individuality." One example of this conformity is the knee-jerk tendency to fall back on adversarial solutions to most, if not all, issues and problems. The young lawyer who sees combativeness as a way of putting her unique stamp on the world is probably taking the least inwardly demanding path to finding out who she really is as a lawyer. Such unexamined behavior has had a devastating impact on collegiality and civility, two much-mourned casualties of contemporary law practice.

True individuality is not imposed from outside; it's a function of who you are. But the burden of perfection that the legal culture places on lawyers tends to inhibit the expression of anything truly their own—which, to the extent that it's real, may feel too rough and unpolished to reveal in the light of day. Worse, by asking you to deny your imperfections—that is, to reject your true self—the culture asks that you deny your own uniqueness.

WHAT'S MISSING?

Caring, compassion, a sense of something greater than the case at hand, a transcendent purpose that gives meaning to your work—these are the legal culture's glaring omissions. It's not that they've been eliminated; in every city and town, there are lawyers who demonstrate the stubborn vitality of values and convictions that will not succumb to widespread aimlessness and cynicism. But to a great extent, such qualities are missing in the academy and in most law firms, and they are conspicuously absent from many lawyers' mental maps. Without them, only one criterion remains by which to measure success, one that has nothing at all to do with your need to do meaningful work or to belong to a profession that stands for something worthwhile: money. Where there is no meaning, at least there is money; where there is no joy, still there is money.

Is it any wonder then that more lawyers are asking themselves why they ever got into this line of work, or, more to the point, what they can do to alleviate their nagging unhappiness? Applications to law schools have generally been stagnant since 1990, and more people than ever are leaving the profession. "I see that the people who the legal profession needs most are leaving because it's sterile territory," says Barbara Reinhold, director of career development at Smith College. "The profession devalues or forbids very important parts of the human experience. In most high-end firms, there is no place for the life of the spirit, only for the life of the mind."

A prominent symptom of the dichotomy Reinhold describes is the current obsession with professionalism. In recent years, leaders of state and national bar associations have undertaken a truly daunting task: to first grasp and then to convey to lawyers what the term is meant to describe. Like nuclear physicists racing to discover a unified field theory that explains the workings of the entire universe and, in a white-hot flash of light, reveals the way ahead, these well-intentioned lawyers have searched their intellectual galaxies for all the available, relevant information. But something appears to be missing, and the great theory continues to elude them.

It wasn't always this way. Not long ago, the concept of professionalism was well understood. It represented a consensus about what it meant to be a lawyer, and it functioned as a kind of cultural glue. In *A Nation Under Lawyers*, Harvard law professor Mary Ann Glendon points out that the concept, as promoted by bar leaders, remained quite stable and clearly understood until the mid-1960s.

That understanding included certain "dependable verities," Glendon notes: that associates who did good work would become partners; that those who did not would be let down easily; that partnership was a reasonably secure status; that independence from clients "could and should be asserted when the occasion required; and that economic considerations would be subordinated, if need arose, to firm solidarity" or to ideals of proper conduct. "Today's lawyers," Glendon goes on to say, "are wandering amidst the ruins of those understandings."

To the lawyers left wandering this landscape of shattered assumptions, all the talk about professionalism seems like so much hot air, for none of the fretting, none of the warnings, none of the hearkening back to the good old days, has helped much. The problem is both deeper and more obvious than that. It has to do with the inner lives of lawyers and, on the collective level, of the entire profession.

At the close of a recent *ABA Journal*–sponsored roundtable discussion on professionalism, William Hoeveler, a federal district judge in Miami, offered a final thought:

> I think one of the basic problems of our profession and all professions is a loss of individual spirituality. This may offend some people, but when I read about the history of this country and the way our Constitution was formed . . . I think about the reasons why lawyers do what they do. And for a lot of them, it is because they have no compass that is directing them. They have no internal direction. And that's becoming more and more pervasive. . . . And this is something we never talk about. We would like to relegate this to the parlors of homes and so forth. But it is a problem that we've got to address and think about. We have lost touch. And I don't care what kind of spiritual values you have—whatever you are is unimportant—but the fact that we are living in an increasingly technological and material world which has no time or room for these thoughts is, I think, one of the deepest problems that we as lawyers face.

Hoeveler is right. Drowned out by the well-intentioned debate on professionalism are the deeper spiritual issues facing lawyers. The challenge to the profession is to honor both the life of the spirit and the life of the mind, and thereby extend the professional map.

Here's one way of looking at it. Every outer reality has an inner correlate: a law-office waiting room is an "outer" reality; a client's comfort level when she enters the space is an inner correlate; a deposition takes place in the external world of action, but a lawyer's intuition that he's taking his client down the wrong road, one that isn't good for her health or psychological well-being, is an inner correlate (among countless other possibilities). In each case, the meaning comes from within, and the texture and depth of that meaning is a function of inner, or spiritual, vitality. In many cases, inner and outer imperatives conflict, such as when the outer culture measures success by hours billed while the inner standard—albeit widely ignored—is hours *lived*, deeply and with awareness.

The problem is that any number of factors have contributed to making lawyers feel painfully unintegrated—not least an almost complete turning away from inner experience. Instead of integration—which you might also think of as balance—separation (imbalance) is very often the hallmark of their experience of the world.

Seven Types of Separation

Disintegration takes various forms, some of them more pernicious than others. In my experience, those that plague lawyers generally fall into seven categories and are expressed as follows:

- Separation from oneself: Having been acculturated to a profession in which adversarial tactics have proliferated beyond litigation into areas that used to be free from such rancor, lawyers lose touch with the more subtle expressions and yearnings of their hearts and minds and come to feel fragmented and often unhealthy. This sense of separation is often measured in the distance they have come from who they once were: sensitive, caring, creative people. Feeling lost, many look to money to create at least a semblance of integration (the surface integration of a cohesive lifestyle), but ultimately a feeling of wholeness is elusive. *"It's so strange. I look successful. I'm told I'm successful. People envy me. And yet I go to bed every night feeling like something is missing, like I haven't done some basic thing that I need to do. I feel incomplete."*

• SEPARATION FROM CLIENTS: Too often, lawyers sense that there are roles to play that preclude real human-to-human contact with clients. (This can be particularly uncomfortable when clients are suffering, as they so often are when they seek a lawyer's help.) Lawyers who feel unintegrated—almost like a collection of thoughts and feelings searching for coherence—have trouble seeing clients as whole people. This is one reason why clients often complain of not feeling heard, seen, or respected by their attorneys. *"Even when they seem happy with the outcome in their cases, I feel like I haven't really connected with them. It makes me sad."*

• SEPARATION FROM THE LAW FIRM: No longer particularly cohesive, law firms are more bottom-line oriented than ever. They tend to support *dis*integration by failing to emphasize the importance of personal growth and career development for partners, associates, and staff, and by rewarding people only for that which can be measured in dollars and cents. *"I feel like a Hollywood actor who is considered only as good as his last movie. It's like that around here. There's a part of you they like, even love, the part they can take to the bank. But there's no place here for the rest of you."*

• SEPARATION FROM FRIENDS AND FAMILY: The stresses of law practice create a great deal of inner turmoil. An inability to express what is going on internally causes a painful sense of separation from the people you care most about. *"We live in separate worlds, my wife and kids and me. I don't want my work life to infect my home life, but there's no way to avoid it. Along with all the battles I've got to endure at work, I've got this internal war going over how best to divide my energy between work and family."*

• SEPARATION FROM LIFE AS PEOPLE LIVE IT: Disintegration is also reflected in a sense of being different, of living apart from "normal" people. Besieged by public antipathy toward their profession, many lawyers feel misunderstood, bewildered, scorned. *"People just don't realize what a double whammy it is to be a lawyer. The public hates you, and meanwhile you're having a hell of a time finding much to like about what you do for a living. Sometimes I just want out, back into a regular job, to no longer be society's whipping boy."*

• SEPARATION FROM THE LAW AS AN EXPRESSION OF SELF IN THE WORLD: This is a sense of being separated from the very purpose of your life. While it might have once seemed as if the law was the ideal vehicle for achieving that purpose (to help people, to advance the cause of justice, to foster economic development, or whatever), many lawyers have resigned themselves to disappointment in the face of a professional reality that doesn't seem to support their personal goals. *"I didn't go to law school to do this!"*

• SEPARATION FROM THE LARGER PROFESSION: This final form is a sense of disenfranchisement, of feeling alienated from a profession that has gone astray and does little to help assuage, or even to acknowledge, lawyers' feelings of separation or promote more balanced lives. *"I'm on my own. I don't really think that, on the organizational level, anyone's got a clue what's wrong."*

Add up these seven types of separation, and what do you get? Legal work that is sterile and inhospitable to the life of the spirit. A legal profession cut off from the larger society. A public that sees the profession as being out of touch with its needs. And lawyers whose isolation and sense of alienation put them at risk for all sorts of physical and emotional problems.

If isolation—or *dis*integration—is dangerous, there is plentiful evidence that an integrative orientation to life is good for your health and well-being. This is perhaps most clear in the area of human relationships, where abundant evidence shows that love and intimacy are the most powerful determinants of health and illness—more than diet, the amount of exercise you get, or whether or not you smoke. Your connectedness with other people, the pioneering cardiologist Dean Ornish has pointed out, affects not only your sense of well-being but also your chances of living a long and healthy life. The flip side of this, Ornish says, is that isolation (that is, "separation") kills.

Milner Ball of the University of Georgia Law School has found a compelling image of integration in a place that most lawyers have probably overlooked. In *Horton Hears a Who*, Dr. Seuss's classic story about the sanctity of all life, only Horton the elephant is capable of hearing the cries of the Whos, a community perched on a tiny dust ball. As those who are deaf to the Whos continually call for the dust ball's destruction, Horton repeatedly reminds them that "a person's a person, no matter how small." In order to hear those Whos—the dispossessed whose calls most of us are not tuned in to—"we first have to hear the Who above us," says Ball. "Because we are on a dust ball too."

Ball is a religious man—in fact, he's an ordained minister—and for him "the Who above us" is no doubt the God in whom he puts his faith.

Hallmarks of *Dis*integration

To feel whole is to feel fully human, able to engage all your capacities and experience a broad range of emotions without overidentifying with any single part of yourself—say, your anger, your need for certainty, or your role as an "important" person. Here are some signs that you may be less integrated, less whole, than you would like:

- You feel like a stranger to yourself. ("I'm forty-seven years old, and I don't feel like I really know myself.")
- You feel that your life is living you, rather than vice versa—the tail is wagging the dog. ("I end the day wondering how I got here, rather than feeling like I made the kind of day that felt right for me.")
- You do not feel particularly aware, moment-to-moment, of your body. ("Other people seem to feel it coming when they get sick. I'm always taken by surprise.")
- You feel out of control of your life, even if—in fact, especially if—you are a controlled and/or controlling person. ("More than anything, I feel as if I'm trying to keep chaos at bay.")
- You rarely, if ever, take time to reflect on the big questions—who you are, how you got here, what you want from life, how satisfied you are with your relationships. ("It would be nice, but I just don't have the time for that.")
- You aren't clear, on a daily basis, that you even *have* an inner life. ("My experience is that I am what I do. Period.")
- You exhibit some kind of compulsive behavior.

But the image is no less compelling from a secular perspective, for instead of merely imagining what the Who above us sees as he or she looks down on us, we can actually see it in the magnificent photographs brought back to us from space. Several astronauts, upon seeing our own staggeringly gorgeous dust ball suspended in deep-black space, report being transformed, having suddenly realized that the integration and wholeness that we all seek is already here. We have only to awaken to it.

NEEDED: A MAP OF THE *WHOLE* WORLD

"Lawyers and law students are invited to believe that the territory mapped out for them at law school is the totality of life," says Charles Halpern, a former law school dean and president until recently of the Nathan Cummings Foundation in New York. "It's not true. There's a real need to fill in the blanks of the map, and spirituality is a big piece of it."

Most lawyers know intuitively that this is true. Some are taking steps to satisfy their hunger for wholeness, to heal the splits that cut them off from their deepest sources of significance and meaning. These lawyers, some of whom you will meet in the coming chapters, are practicing integration. They are living out a set of deeply held personal values or, put another way, hewing to their own spiritual paths. Some are consciously pursuing a working model of law practice that, as one Florida litigator has said, is based on the understanding that lawyer, client, opponent, and legal system are all part of a single whole, the great web of life. And they are actively seeking meaning, even as they rack up their billables and put out clients' fires.

It's important to remember that people really can change. Oliver Wendell Holmes himself is a great example. The very same man who thought that perhaps the law ought to be cleansed of all its moral content—though now in his nineties—put this advice in a letter to a young man just embarking on a legal career: "For your sake I hope that when your work seems to present only mean details, you may realize that every detail has the mystery of the universe behind it and may keep your heart with an undying faith." On another occasion he maintained that no other profession "gives such scope to realize the spontaneous energy of one's soul."

When a profession demands as much as the law does on most days, it is hard to imagine where you can find the time and mental space to attend to your split-off parts, invite more of yourself into your work, and nurture the deep pleasure that law practice still can offer. Increasingly, the answer must be *at work* as well as at home, with colleagues, with clients, and in your own—and your law firm's—relationships with your community. If not, with so much of your time being spent at work or recovering from work, dispiritedness is almost inevitable.

Integration can be cultivated. People have done it for millennia, using a wide variety of practices, many of which can be tailored to the life of a busy lawyer. The bottom line is this: You can have a vibrant inner life, one that nourishes your professional life so that what you *do* becomes more of an expression of who you *are*. It can be a kind of homecoming, a return to a place that feels familiar yet utterly new. It can bring excitement back to your law practice.

Feeling Whole

It isn't easy to pin down what it means to be whole or integrated. But it's worth trying. Here are some qualities or experiences that may give at least a hint of what the desired state is all about:

- You have a sense of diversity in your life—diversity of feelings, thoughts, and experiences. In social and biological systems, diversity is a sign of strength and vibrancy. So it is in individuals, who atrophy when they become emotionally and intellectually monochromatic. Great strength, and a sense of harmony, comes from the unfettered interplay of intellect, spirit, and emotions.
- You are able to articulate, to your own satisfaction, what matters to you and what principles guide you in your life. You live in harmony with them, both at work and at home.
- You see your work as a servant of your values, passions, and sense of purpose in life.
- You are emotionally open and—at least in some circumstances—able to laugh with gusto, to cry, to be real.
- When you are angry, you are aware of it and you take responsibility for it, rather than making it someone else's fault.

This isn't just theory or wishful thinking. The same integrative/holistic awareness that has emerged in medicine and is now getting attention in business and education has gained a foothold in the legal world. Let's take a look at some lawyers whose inner maps are changing as they strive to recover from the disintegration that the legal culture has encouraged.

CHAPTER TWO

INTEGRATING YOUR HEART AND MIND

The search for meaning does not require us to throw out analytic reasoning, but it does suggest embodying logic with heart and passion.

—*Alan Briskin*

The Stirring of Soul in the Workplace

THE FIVE-YEAR-OLD SAID IT.

He had been in the courtroom for the entire trial, three days in the front row of the visitor's gallery with his older brothers and sisters. All five were orphans now that a car accident had taken their mother away. Wounded into silence, the youngest sat through it all—through the lawyers' openings, through detailed expert testimony and accident reconstructions—never saying a word. Only waiting.

When the lawyers finally made their closing remarks, he sensed that maybe the wait would end soon. All their talk of "wrongful death," "liability," and "preponderance of evidence" meant nothing. He needed an answer.

So did Irwin Stolz. The lawyer for the mother's estate, Stolz wanted to do right by the kids. Regardless of what they got—assuming the jury found in the estate's favor—their road through life was not going to be easy. The best he could hope for was to provide some damage control. Money could help some, maybe ease the pain just a little. He finished his closing and began preparing for the worst, while hoping for the best.

When the Rome, Georgia, jury finally filed back into the courtroom, Stolz, at the counsel table, was intensely aware of the five stony faces directly behind him. The foreman read the verdict: *for the plaintiff,* and Stolz was flooded with a sense of relief; now he could turn and face the children without hesitation.

The little boy was already standing. As Stolz left the well, the child approached. He looked up with big, needy eyes.

"Does this mean my mama didn't do anything wrong?" he asked.

Stolz began to cry. "It just tore me up," he recalls, years later. "You try to do the best you can, and here it turns out that all that time he'd thought that maybe his mother had done something wrong."

Not everyone is as lucky as Stolz was that day. He found meaning in his work—meaning that touched him deeply—beyond what law school and his years of practice had prepared him to see. In the eyes of that five-year-old, he found something that opened his own eyes: not only could he do some "damage control," but he also had the opportunity to heal this little boy's heart and free him to go on with the process of grieving.

Stolz, a former state appeals court judge and now a name partner in an Atlanta law firm, is well known in state legal circles as a fine lawyer and a compassionate man. But he knows you have to work to stay that way, to preserve your soul in a culture that values winning to the exclusion of almost everything else. The boy in Rome was one of many teachers who have sensitized him—who he has *allowed* to sensitize him—to the different roles a lawyer can play in our society.

Irwin Stolz isn't the only lawyer around who has had a transforming experience without consciously working toward that goal. Sometimes it happens when a parent or a spouse dies, or when a child becomes seriously ill. These events bring forgotten feelings and intuitions, along with a great outpouring of love, into awareness. Things become clearer than they've ever been, and suddenly the road ahead is plain. The effect on a law practice can be profound. "I could not go back to what I had been doing," remarks one lawyer, describing how she felt in the days and weeks after being at her mother's side when she died. "I could not put my armor back on and go out and fight." She has not been in a courtroom for years.

Sheldon Tashman, a sole practitioner in New York City, had what he calls "a peak experience" several years ago after finishing a project that had been unusually difficult, hard, and long. It had required him to do work he had never done before, including putting together an innovative deal and selling the concept to potential investors. It had gone extremely well.

After six weeks of nonstop work, he took a week off. He recalls the night at a resort when he put his head down on the pillow and everything changed. In his mind, Tashman saw himself flying over a desert, onto which he could see a light shining down, illuminating a path. But from his vantage point, he could see that there "was no one right path. There were many ways to get across the desert." Next, he saw a large dam. Cracks began forming in it, and suddenly water came crashing down.

When he woke up the next morning, things were different. "One of the first signs that something had changed at a deep level was that my tastes in food were different," he remembers. "It was amazing. And my relationships changed. I was living far more consciously than I ever had."

Instead of worrying about his spot on the ladder of success, for the first time in his life Tashman was able to accept himself as he was. "I had this wonderful feeling of well-being," he recalls. "And, at the same time, people started gravitating to me for the first time. It was because I was different; I didn't have an agenda. I was just with them. I would walk down the street and see things in people—particularly pain and discomfort. It all became so clear to me. I had never had this sense before of really *feeling* how other people felt."

Although the feeling didn't last, Tashman promised himself he would remember and build on it from then on. And he has. "Because it has remained in my memory, I have been able to rebuild a place in myself to nurture the concepts that felt so fundamental." Since his experience at the resort, his sense of purpose has become clearer, and practicing in a way that is consistent with his values has become the only way he *can* practice. He has become a better, more caring, and vastly more fulfilled lawyer—a fact that friends and colleagues talk about with admiration.

One final defining moment: a lawyer in his fifties, outwardly successful, with a small law firm in the Sunbelt. In recent years, he had found it harder and harder to deny realities that he had shut out for decades, particularly the sorry state of his family relationships and the looming inevitability of death. He began to feel certain that at some point he would have to confront his fears directly. Still, he put it off.

As with Tashman, something happened while he was on vacation. It may have been his deepening sense of relaxation or being alone with his wife in a quiet place with few distractions—something he hadn't done for a long time—but something opened up inside of him and he was able to talk to her about his feelings and, for once, not feel the need to hide from his fears. They talked for hours about things that he had, until that day, resigned himself to shouldering alone. After that, change wasn't an option; it was the only possibility.

When he returned to the office, he wasted no time telling his partners what had happened. Noticing tears in their eyes, he became aware that he wasn't the only one wrestling with such feelings. Together, over time and with great dedication, they worked out a new way of approaching things, of relating to life not only as individuals and as lawyers, but also as a group. They decided to talk on a regular basis. To check in. Reconnect. Allow themselves the luxury—which they realized really wasn't a luxury at all—of being real with each other. A moment had come for all of them when it became clear that there was really no other way to go on.

An epiphany led each of these lawyers to seek ways to find and cultivate meaning in their lives and to rediscover their own humanity. They are among those who are beginning to realize that when a sense of the ineffable is present, then awe and even joy begin to creep into the workday—better gifts to take home than the usual frustration and exhaustion. Athletes, artists, writers—like everyone else, they seek moments of transcendence, times when things just click, when they are "in the zone" and suddenly the seamlessness of reality is revealed. It can happen in law practice too, if you are sufficiently open to experience to allow such gloriously altered states of consciousness to seize you and send you soaring.

OVERCOMING DOMAIN-BOUND THINKING

Happy or not, lawyers tend to be proud of their skills, both those they acquired in law school and those that can come only from years in practice. And justifiably so. No other profession comes close to the law in preparing people to take on a wide variety of challenges, whether in the practice of law, business, politics, or journalism. Some of it has to do with the simple fact that lawyers know how to get things done. Their analytical skills are superb, they are skilled negotiators, and they can quickly size up a situation and draw the right inferences.

But many lawyers make a crucial error by failing to acknowledge that some problems resist left-brain solutions and that the intellect isn't the only tool available with which to address their own or their clients' problems. Because of a heavy investment in their intellectual prowess, they resist the notion that spirituality may have something to do with their dilemma. Like actors who refer to their voices as their "instrument" and assiduously guard against anything that might imperil it, they feel concerned about getting involved in issues beyond the solid, clear, analyzable dimension they are used to—lest it fog their analytical lenses and muddy their thinking.

This is a valid concern but also a very lawyerly one. It's "us v. them" thinking. It leads to the natural conclusion that a "spiritual" mind-set— one that can measure "the swerve, or the inclination of the soul," to borrow a phrase from the novelist Joyce Carol Oates—is something for other people, fuzzy-headed folks with time to contemplate their navels in incense-filled rooms. Lawyers, on the other hand, have to be tough-minded and nimble. They have neither the time or any obvious reason to develop an inner life or to ponder the invisible. The implication is that the two modes of thought—or perhaps more accurately, the two types of intelligence—are antithetical and that, where lawyers are concerned, the twain should never meet.

Although hard data on the complementarity of different modes of intelligence are not yet available, scientists have considered the question. Mihaly Csikszentmihalyi, the eminent University of Chicago professor of human development and education and author of *Flow*, says it is his opinion, and that of several other research psychologists, that our very survival as a people requires that we integrate our thinking.

While "specialized domain-bound thinking" is necessary in a world dominated by specialization, Csikszentmihalyi believes that too much specialization may imperil us. "Unless a certain fraction of our thinking, both as individuals and as a culture, is devoted to monitoring the state of the system as a whole—the ecology, the polity, the community—we are likely to fall apart as a people. We are getting increasingly differentiated cognitively, but without cognitive integration, entropy is likely to prevail." Without doubt, lawyers have a special social function, a unique role to play in what Csikszentmihalyi refers to as the system as a whole.

"Think about an orchestra. You can hear the trumpets, but you're aware of the whole orchestra at the same time," says Stephen Chakwin, a veteran New York litigator. "I've tried to do that in my practice, and it has led to many successes. If you understand the big picture, in which the small details matter, you can understand how and why they matter, and you can explain it to others. When you look at things through a spiritual dimension, nothing says you have to turn the focus dial all the way to one side."

The problem is that the dial has been turned too far the other way, away from the kind of inner understanding that is rooted in connectedness and relationship. As Alan Briskin puts it in his book *The Stirring of Soul in the Workplace*, logic becomes "the thin crust that suppresses meaning rather than fostering its awakening within the individual." The result is a gap between the professional and the human being, along with amnesia about the essential identity of the two. The great challenge, then, is to return to a concept of work as it has been understood in spiritual traditions for millennia—that is, as an activity in which the inner and outer lives come together in a meaningful engagement with the world.

But it can be tough. During the last two decades, the legal profession has placed an increasingly heavy emphasis on efficiency, on working "smarter" and faster. It makes demands not only on your outer life—in constant deadlines, billable-hour quotas, pressure to keep up with a rapidly growing body of new law—but on your inner life as well. The problem is that most lawyers have never developed the resources to cope with those demands, let alone find in them the kind of meaning that can make their work more rewarding. They hear only the blare of the trumpet and miss the sonority of an orchestra that can provide resonance and depth.

To find real pleasure in the legal life, you need to open yourself to all your sources of potential meaning. You will discover that understanding a client beyond her present legal problem does not detract from the technical job at hand; it gives the technical job deeper meaning by placing it in the context of a life. Contracts, after all, are about human relationships; briefs are about disappointment, wanting to be heard, needing to heal. Seeing these deeper meanings is not a threat to good work; it enriches the experience of doing the work, engages the lawyer's heart, and makes the end product more likely to be compelling.

One model for what it might look like to live a legal life infused with the energies of the heart and the spirit is that of Mohandas K. Gandhi. Gandhi worked constantly, throughout his life, and yet he maintained an uncanny ability to see the spiritual dimension in even the most mundane activities—sweeping floors, spinning yarn—and in unpleasant conditions, such as prison. And he was clear about the implications for his law practice: "I understood that the true function of a lawyer was to unite parties riven asunder," he wrote. "The lesson was so indelibly burnt into me that a large part of my time during the twenty years of my practice was occupied in bringing about private compromises of hundreds of cases. I lost nothing thereby—not even money, certainly not my soul." Awareness of the entire orchestra became, for Gandhi, a way of life.

Not only can such an awareness add texture and richness to your work and make it that much more rewarding, but also you can rest assured that it represents a kind of integration that your clients need. David Hall of Northeastern University speaks as a client when he says, "When I go to a lawyer, I want something more than just legal advice. I mean, when I go to the grocery store to buy a loaf of bread, I hope to be treated a certain way by the cashier. If she doesn't put the money in my hand and acknowledge me, I feel diminished by that. So I don't want a caring lawyer who can't write a good brief, but at the same time, I don't want a lawyer who can write a very good brief yet he can't hear me. He can't understand me and my story, and can't be there with me as I'm going through a difficult experience."

THE PATH TO CHANGE: SPIRITUAL PRACTICE

For most lawyers, the word *practice* means only one thing: work. You are, after all, *practitioners.* You practice law, and you are in the practice of providing legal services. With all the practicing you do, it may come as a surprise that you are profoundly in need of a second practice, one that gives greater depth to the first.

The purpose of this secondary practice is to bring out the best in you and help you get to know parts of yourself that have been overlooked or pushed aside in response to the demands of a frantic professional life.

It will move you toward wholeness, toward accepting yourself for all that you are, so that you can bring your heart and soul to work, find the joy in it, and have more left to give to others.

But it's also about taking care of yourself, not in the sense of indulging your desires for bigger and better things, but by nurturing your deepest needs—for peace, love, meaning, and a certain quality of presence. If you are like most lawyers, self-nurturing doesn't come easy to you. You work tirelessly to meet everyone else's needs—clients, staff, family, the bar association—in what feels like a never-ending battle to cover your flanks and keep bad news at bay. Despite all the talk of avaricious lawyers, you end up feeling impoverished.

Only you can say what is truly nurturing for you. It may be taking a walk in the park, soaking in a hot bath, putting aside a few minutes for personal reflection, or spending a week in silent retreat. Perhaps it's playing a set of tennis, watching your dogs frolic, listening to a Bach cello suite, or carefully threading a necklace of colorful beads. It really doesn't matter what it is, as long as you engage in it fully, with not just your head but also your heart.

For countless centuries and throughout the world, some kind of spiritual practice was seen as an essential tool for educating the inner person, a basic ingredient in the experience of being human. These were time-tested methods for quieting the mind and accessing truths and levels of understanding that profoundly enhance even the most mundane activities of daily life. If playing golf happens to make you feel at one with the world, keep doing it. But there are other practices, most of which take much less time on a daily basis than a round of golf, that can enhance your relationships and deepen your enjoyment of your law practice (as well as your golf game).

A Common Message

Here, the great religions of the world have much to teach, whether or not you are comfortable with their outward trappings. In his book *Grace and Grit*, philosopher Ken Wilber distinguishes between "exoteric" and "esoteric" religion. Exoteric or "outer" religion, he explains, "is mythic religion, religion that is terribly concrete and literal, that really believes, for example, that Moses parted the Red Sea, that Krishna made love to four thousand cow maidens, that the world was created in six days, and so on." These "belief structures," says Wilber, "attempt to explain the mysteries of the world in mythic terms rather than direct experiential or evidential terms." In their fundamentalist forms, these religions insist that salvation comes only when one accepts the full panoply of myths as they have been handed down through the ages.

Esoteric religion, on the other hand, involves direct experience and personal awareness. This "inner" form of religion "asks you to believe nothing on faith or obediently swallow any dogma," Wilber says. "Rather, [it] is a set of personal experiments that you conduct scientifically in the laboratory of your own awareness. Like all good science it is based on direct experience, not mere belief or wish, and it is publicly checked and validated by a peer group of those who have also performed the experiment." After about six millennia of this experiment, says Wilber, "we are perfectly justified in making certain conclusions, making certain spiritual theorems, as it were. And those spiritual theorems are the core of the perennial wisdom traditions."

The really extraordinary thing about esoteric, or mystical, spiritual experiences is that—unlike exoteric religions, which are all quite different from one another—they are virtually identical. Fundamentally, they agree on the nature of the soul and the spirit.

The distinction between these fundamental spiritual modes, exoteric and esoteric, is crucial, in an age of skepticism, when people—particularly educated, analytical people—are looking for something with an empirical basis upon which to hang their spiritual yearnings. Whether the method is meditation, contemplative prayer, mindfulness practice, contemplation of nature, or certain focused artistic practices, there is a huge written record attesting to their efficacy in deepening personal understanding of what it means to be human. The source may be Plotinus, Plato, Augustine, Meister Eckhart, Sri Auribindo, the Baal Shem Tov, or a living master such as the Dalai Lama, but the messages are, at bottom, the same. They reveal our interrelatedness—that is, the illusory quality of our separateness—and the sacredness of all things. For anyone who respects the legal doctrine of *stare decisis*, here is an approach to spirituality that offers an extraordinarily large body of precedent.

Whole Person, Whole Lawyer

The goal of all spiritual practice is summed up nicely in these words by the writer Ellen Bass: "There's a part of every living thing that wants to become itself, the tadpole into the frog, the chrysalis into the butterfly, a damaged human being into a whole one. That is spirituality."

This brings up a crucial question: When you are most yourself— that is, when you feel most authentic and alive—how does that affect the way you experience practicing law? If you can't answer this question but wish you could—that is, if you sense that in the answer is something deeply important to you—the following seven chapters should strike a nerve.

The people in these chapters have brought their law practices into stronger alignment with their innermost values, each in his or her own way. In most cases, they didn't have a sudden flash of awareness, like Tashman. Nor are you likely to; nor do you need to. That's what spiritual practices are for. All of the practices that follow work, at least on one level, by restoring some semblance of balance in the relationship between the inner life and the outer life. The trick with any of them is to be patient and to realize the truth in the old adage that says it is the path, rather than the destination, that matters most. In the path is the meaning, the joy, and the mystery—as well as the answer to the question posed earlier: What kind of lawyer are you when you are most yourself, most awake, most whole?

The following seven chapters look at how lawyers are using various practices to help bring heart, mind, and spirit into harmony in order to heighten their awareness of what their *real* work is. Though their emphases are somewhat different, they all have certain things in common, including an accent on:

- cultivating awareness and using it to see more deeply
- awakening to the inner life so that eventually it will find expression in all that you do
- acting intentionally in the world rather than simply reacting to circumstances
- finding the beautiful, the sacred, the meaningful in life's everyday events and experiences

"The Balanced Practice," "The Contemplative Practice," "The Mindful Practice," and "The Service Practice" are classic spiritual practices, brought up-to-date in the lives of the lawyers who use them. The others—"The Time-Out Practice," "The Listening Practice," and

"The Healing Practice"—are a bit more eclectic, suggesting mind-sets, or orientations toward work and life, that confer spiritual, emotional, and professional benefits on the practitioner. See which ones work for you, then make the time to try them on a regular basis.

These practices will help you move toward seeing the world whole, so that you might personally and professionally work to support its wholeness. They will give you the tools you need to become aware of your own essential wholeness, by helping you to suspend criticism and judgment—not easy for anyone; really tough for lawyers, for whom the critical faculty reigns supreme. Unless you find a way to do it, though, you will continue to experience yourself as fragmented, the island that is your rational mind cut off from the subsurface depths.

When you become free, even for minutes at a time, from the need to hide from your own critical barbs, you can start to become aware of the parts of yourself that have been split off or disowned. You can then begin to reclaim them and slowly reclaim your oneness—that is, the inner experience of integrity. In a similar way, when you allow friends, family members, or clients this same freedom, they too can begin to unfold in your presence and let you know who they are, not just as "wife," "old pal," or "medmal suit," for example, but as people.

With commitment to a practice, you will begin to reap extraordinary personal and professional benefits. Commitment itself, as wise people have long remarked, has a way of opening up possibilities and making things happen. Goethe put it this way: ". . . the moment one definitely commits oneself, then Providence moves too. A whole stream of events issues from the decision, raising in one's favor all manner of unforeseen incidents and meetings and material assistance, which no [man] could ever dream would come his way."

PART TWO

VOYAGE OF
DISCOVERY

*The only effort worth making is the one it takes
to learn the geography of one's own nature.*
—Paul Frederick Bowles

CHAPTER THREE

THE BALANCED PRACTICE

My life is not this steeply sloping hour,
in which you see me hurrying.
—*Rainer Maria Rilke*

ACHIEVING BALANCE IS A PRACTICE. It's a challenge and a necessity. When you are out of balance—that is, when you give significantly more attention to one part of yourself than to others—you feel it. You may become fearful, like a child on the raised end of a seesaw, whose exhilaration can't overcome the knowledge that there is a long way to fall. And a painful bump at the end. Or you may find yourself trying to believe that your success in one area—your work, for example—compensates for your lack of attention to other areas, say, your relationships or your physical and emotional health. And likely as not, you will come to feel less effective in every part of your life, even the one that claims most of your energy.

Practicing balance, like practicing law, is an ongoing affair. You don't just get it, close the file, and move on to other things. You *keep* practicing. You get better, wiser, more sensitive to nuance.

If you sense that your life is out of balance and that healing of some kind is needed, the experience of Memphis lawyer John McQuiston II may be instructive. He discovered—or perhaps it is more accurate to say that he let life teach him—the importance of being open to healing influences wherever they are to be found. And McQuiston found them in a most unlikely place: a set of directions for running a monastery, written in the sixth century by an Italian monk.

McQuiston was a typically busy commercial litigator in March 1991 when his father died. The two had been particularly close, as McQuiston was an only child and had lost his mother at the age of fifteen. Returning to Birmingham, Alabama, for the funeral, he met an Episcopal priest who had been a good friend and golfing partner of his father.

They got along well and spent hours talking. McQuiston found himself confiding in the priest, sharing the vexing questions that were foremost in his mind after his loss: What is it we're here to accomplish, and is accomplishment really even the point of life? The priest recommended a book he thought might be helpful. It was about the Rule of St. Benedict.

McQuiston wasn't quite ready to pursue the suggestion. At the time, he was one of two primary rainmakers at a ten-lawyer firm, a firm he had joined in the early '70s, when he was a self-described hyperachiever just out of Vanderbilt law school. Only one other lawyer at the firm was under fifty-five, and as the years passed and the ranks of older lawyers thinned out, McQuiston's share of responsibility had increased. Throughout the 1980s and into the early '90s, he felt as if the weight of the entire firm were on his shoulders. "The demands on my time were infinite, and the time I had was finite," he says. "I think a lot of lawyers get themselves into that position."

But things changed in 1991. Not only did he lose his father, but five months later his firm merged with another law firm. Overnight, he became one of seven or eight rainmakers in a twenty-lawyer firm. "Suddenly, I could take a deep breath," he says.

The following summer, he and his family spent a week in a dormitory on the grounds of Canterbury Cathedral in England. It was there that St. Benedict showed up again, this time when he met people who knew the author of the book the priest had recommended back in Birmingham.

McQuiston went out and bought a copy of the Rule. "I did the good, lawyerlike thing and went straight to the source document, rather than just read *about* it," he recalls. What he found in the thin red volume was a set of guidelines for monastic life that would apply, in large measure, to running a boys' school: directions for establishing sleeping arrangements, organizing meals, managing the institution's money, and so on. Other parts could apply only to a religious institution, such as the requirement that monks attend church seven times a day.

In this ancient text, McQuiston found something he needed: "The idea of taking control of my daily life to have time for meditation, or prayer, or peace and quiet, or study was something that drove me to the Rule of St. Benedict." It was an idea he had harbored for some time, only now he had the time to do something about it. It's not that he wasn't working hard. He was. But he no longer felt totally responsible for keeping his firm afloat.

And he had already established a precedent that put him in an unusual position *vis-à-vis* the Rule. He had previously rewritten the Episcopal service of morning prayer so that, he says, it would speak to him as it once had. Each morning he took some quiet time to read from *his* version of the service, and soon he began including readings from the Rule of St. Benedict.

Then he began adapting the Rule, working every Saturday morning "to free its underlying methods and principles from their original context and terminology to make them relevant" for him. McQuiston was drawn to the process primarily because he thought he'd enjoy it, but also for the balance he was sure it would add to his life. It did just that, by providing a counterweight to the pressures of his practice, while also allowing him to use his legal skills in a way that satisfied his spiritual yearnings.

"I was trying to say if St. Benedict was alive today and was living in this culture and was trying to tell me, John McQuiston, something about how to live, how would he say it?"

This, McQuiston points out, is something lawyers do all the time: take a principle from one set of facts and try to apply it to a different set of facts. His legal training, he says, helped him bring the Rule into the twentieth century.

Although McQuiston rewrote the Rule for himself, friends convinced him to send it to a publisher. In 1996, it was published by Morehouse Press as *Always We Begin Again: The Benedictine Way of Living*. "Being a lawyer, I wanted to call it 'The Rule of St. Benedict Restated,' but the publisher didn't go for that," he says.

The Benedictine Quest for Balance

In a way, McQuiston's decision to restate the Rule of St. Benedict echoes Benedict's own purpose for writing the Rule. With the Rule, Benedict designed a way of life defined by standards that went against the prevailing culture, one that he saw as irreverent and venal. McQuiston too sought to create something that offered him an alternative to *his* culture, and not only the culture of America in the 1990s, but also the culture of law.

"Lawyers are people who desperately need balance and some boundaries on their personal time," he says, adding that Benedictine monks have a specific daily routine that speaks to that need. "They try to have a bit of everything. Time for learning. Time for prayer. Time for companionship, and so on." Benedict's genius, McQuiston says, was in his understanding of the value of habit, that by changing the way we behave and think, we change our lives. "This is why you can start out doing something mechanically, not exactly knowing where you're going, and still end up with some benefits."

In the preface to *Always We Begin Again*, McQuiston explains why he finds the Rule relevant today:

> [It] teaches that if we take control of our lives, if we are intentional
> and careful in how we spend the hours of each irreplaceable day, if we
> discipline ourselves to live in a balanced and thankful way, we will cre-
> ate from our experiences, whatever they may be, the best possible life.
> Surely this knowledge is as invaluable now as it was in the sixth century.

It has certainly proven its relevance in his life.

"For me, the Rule came as things do that come into people's lives in a serendipitous way," he says. "You have a need you don't even recognize, and something comes along and fills it." What McQuiston needed was the kind of healing that comes from a restoration of balance, not just the work-life/family-life kind of balance with which most lawyers are so familiar, but also the balancing of one's inner and outer selves. The depth of that need is reflected in his determination to find personal meaning in a rather opaque ancient text and to flush out its relevance to modern life.

McQuiston's version of the Rule secularizes concepts that originated in a deeply religious setting. "We all have our own perception of, in law firms is worrisome to many. With the quality of lawyering often taking a backseat to the relentless pursuit of ever more billable hours, Bachman has arrived at this rather frightening formulation: "Ten percent of a lawyer's soul dies for every 100 billable hours worked in excess of 1,500 per year."

That adds up to a lot of dead or dying souls. It explains a lot too. In order to have any kind of moral or spiritual life, you need time now and then to reflect on things, to step back from the gears and see the entire clock. Without having some kind of consciousness about the big picture, you slog on—making money, yes, but growing not a whit; missing out on the pleasures of friendship and intimacy; stacking up hours like bricks in a wall, until most of what matters has been sealed out.

The billable hour makes more challenging the cultivation of a spiritual life, or the development of any kind of inner life. Its demands and lack of flexibility lead even accomplished professionals to feel enslaved, trapped in lavishly furnished cells in which the door is wide open but escape feels impossible. It can seem so inimical to the integration of mind, body, and spirit that it is hard to feel hopeful about overcoming its effects.

"Working fifty-, sixty-, seventy-hour weeks will, by definition, desensitize you as a human being," says Rob Ricken, a litigator and matrimonial attorney in Kingston, New York. "You're going to gain billable hours and make more money, but I question whether you're going to deliver much quality to clients—and to your family and your friends."

His solution is to limit his workweek to four days, and to take time off to do what he likes—hiking in the mountains, working with animals, and being with his family. He brings the sense of balance this gives him to work, where he is able to think more clearly on behalf of his clients. It also helps him enjoy better relationships with his wife, his children, his parents, and his community.

Ricken, who tries hard to remember to be thankful for what he has, says that freeing himself from the oppression of the billable hour has been liberating, though it remains a struggle. "I cut my own firewood, and I split it and stack it," he says. "It takes a tremendous amount of effort to accumulate five cords of wood for the winter. Now I could buy the same amount of wood for $500. That amounts to two and a half hours of my legal work. If I look at it from the point of view of dollars and cents, I will follow the path that most lawyers do—their

and relationship to, some God," McQuiston writes. "We may not use the name 'God.' We may think in terms of Reality, Nature, The First Cause, The Behavior of the World, The Other, The All, The Ground of Being, The Force of Evolution, The Life Spirit, or Things as They Really Are. Each of us creates an image of the supreme mystery in which we find ourselves, and we are always in a relationship with it." McQuiston's vision clearly transcends his own spiritual tradition as well as Benedict's and reaches out to the universal human need to be in relationship with something greater than ourselves.

Another example of modernizing the Rule is what McQuiston does with an original passage on managing the monastery's finances. In a section entitled "Stewardship," he extrapolates from the original, offering a series of insightful observations, all of them highly relevant today. "At all times let us recall that every thing which we use in this life was here before us and will be here after we are gone. This world and everything in it is on loan, entrusted to our care for our time," he writes. This too is a lesson in balance: Remembering the source of our true wealth helps keep us grateful and humble in our relationship to the world and to each other. And on those days when it feels as if practicing law is ultimately a matter of eating or being eaten, it may be comforting to remember the big picture and the vital role you play in it.

Working the Rule

For lawyers, the proof ultimately is in the practice, and McQuiston insists that living a more balanced life, in which every day is planned to include a variety of rewarding activities, has made his practice more enjoyable than ever. "I'm not overcommitted anymore. I don't have the same stress level," he says. "Practicing law, for those who enjoy it, can be addictive. It's really a question of realizing there are other things in life that are rewarding."

For McQuiston, following the Rule of St. Benedict has not only practical but also spiritual benefits, which in turn have affected his practice. "I think I now have a deeper spiritual life, but it isn't the kind where I could make a list of what I believe. It's not a formula or a creed; it's a comfort level with existence, a trust in the cosmos. I have a deeper sense that I belong here and that I'm doing what fits for me."

As a practical matter, this spiritual deepening has made McQuiston more relaxed and flexible with clients. He's now more willing to bring "a broad perspective of values" to his law practice than he was trained to do, and he gives advice and offers recommendations about what clients should or shouldn't do much more readily than before. He'll help them see their cases from outside the narrow perspective of law, and he has no qualms about questioning whether litigation is the way to go. "I'll ask, 'What's your best judgment? Do you really think the game is worth the candle?'" Not only don't his clients mind his new attitude, but he's been pleased to find that they welcome "absolute, ruthless candor."

The reason McQuiston now finds it easier to counsel clients in a different way—to suggest, for example, that a lawsuit may not be in the client's best interest—is simple: "If every morning you get up and spend a little time reading or meditating or thinking about the forest in the ultimate sense—in other words, looking at the big picture—it seeps into your consciousness, and it doesn't go away during the day. Well, it may. But it comes back again."

Living the kind of life he does, McQuiston acknowledges, requires getting comfortable with the idea of making less money. "You don't necessarily *make* less money—last year I had my best year ever—but you have to be comfortable with the possibility. If it happens that you do well, it happens; but that's not the objective. For me, the only monetary objective is to make enough to run the family. Beyond that, it's lagniappe. It's gravy.

"One of my favorite lines in the book is something I took from the Tao Te Ching," McQuiston says. "It says that the only person who is really wealthy is the one who thinks he has enough."

For McQuiston, the overall effect of living a contemporary version of the Benedictine way has been to integrate all the parts of his life—his need to contemplate the divine as he conceives it, to study, to spend time with family and friends, and to play (he enjoys golf). Such integration is intrinsically healing because it has reconnected him with parts of himself that had long been pushed aside—and it has helped him realize that there are things beyond work that are, in and of themselves, inherently worthwhile.

"Lawyers need to realize that their time is a lot more valuable than the money they're making with it," he says. "The guy who says, 'I'm making $200 an hour; I'd better stay here for another hour' has got his values exactly backwards."

 Ominous Signs

Many people who are in a chronic state of imbalance are not aware of it. Having lacked a sense of equilibrium for so long, they no longer realize that their deprivation is neither normal nor healthy. And they miss what may very well be staring them in the face: that they have become distorted, sometimes even grotesque—certainly not the whole people they were born to be.

Certain signs of imbalance are fairly obvious, at least when we see them in others. For example:

- working too much
- spending most, if not all, waking hours in intellectual pursuits
- neglecting the body and ignoring the importance of physical well-being
- having rapid mood swings
- making play into work—that is, taking leisure activities too seriously or becoming overcompetitive
- neglecting friends and family
- failing to take time for quiet reflection

Other indicators are somewhat less obvious, but nonetheless indicate a problem, such as:

- spending too much time thinking about the past or the future and too little time being aware of the present moment
- eating unconsciously, without concern for whether you are really hungry or how your food tastes
- sleeping too little or too much
- frequently feeling restless or irritable
- rarely or never being aware of the sacred in the everyday
- frequently going to bed at night feeling that somehow your day was incomplete

BATTLING THE BILLABLE THREAT

Minnesota lawyer Walt Bachman, author of *Law v. Life: What Lawyers Are Afraid to Say About the Legal Profession*, speaks for many lawyers when he confesses that he has a clearer memory of the time sheets he kept when he began practicing law than of his oldest child's first words. The steady rise in recent years of the minimum number of hours required

decisions are economically based. But you have to base your decisions on quality of life. You can't buy that. Still, life is a constant struggle to keep the balance."

Another way Ricken combats the effects of billable-hour mind, as a Zen master might call it, is to consciously and deliberately shift his mental and emotional rhythm when he gets home from work. He takes a half hour alone, to change his clothes, sit quietly, and resensitize himself to the world of home and family. "It's not like I leave my work and go home to life, or leave my life and go to work," he says. "It's all one life. But as much spirit as I try to bring to work, I am still a warrior at times. So office consciousness and home consciousness are just different. Taking the time helps me start to head in a different direction. It balances me."

Ricken brings an awareness of time's preciousness into his work, too, where he sometimes asks clients who are in an attack mode to reflect on what their time is worth to them. "I'll say to them, 'If you end up getting x number of dollars, then you've got to think about what the value of your misery is for the two years you'll be fighting this thing.'"

What he is doing is combining the role of adversary with other roles lawyers can play (not including the "hired gun"), and thereby maintaining a certain balance in his work. Depending on the case, he can be a trusted counselor, a confidant, a healer, or even a mentor, as when he occasionally represents juvenile offenders. Confining himself to any one role would be to court imbalance, monotony, and disaffection for the practice. For any lawyer, each case is a balancing act, an opportunity to define a connection that feels right for both client and attorney. Seeking balance within a law practice is to move toward greater effectiveness and satisfaction and to open the door to a joyful professional life.

Like McQuiston, who found fulfillment in living a modern-day Benedictine life, Ricken says that achieving balance is ultimately about "realizing you don't need that much stuff." It's a realization that, if it is allowed to sink in, is tremendously healing. It makes so many things possible again—lazy walks with loved ones, reading, contemplation, giving something back to the community—and it provides a chance to make peace with the clock and to see the true value of time. It puts life in perspective.

"When people ask me what I do, I realize that I shovel manure more than anything else," says Ricken, who raises horses, cows, and llamas on his farm in Woodstock, New York. "I do a lot of things. A lot of lawyers define themselves as lawyers. They gain their identities from it. Lawyering is just one part of my life, one of many pieces."

Transforming Your Practice

Practicing balance means paying attention to what makes you feel whole, becoming aware of what you're neglecting, and giving overemphasized parts of yourself a well-deserved break. In a culture that often glorifies *im*balance in the practitioners it holds up as role models, it is crucial to remember that only you can know what makes you feel balanced and what it might take to get there.

Here are a number of ways you might move toward balance in your life:

- Spend some time thinking about what parts of yourself you're neglecting. Your body? Your spiritual side? Your need for friendship, love, or intimacy? Your need for connection with your past and your life story?
- Take ten minutes each morning to think about the big picture. Readings from books on spirituality can be helpful.
- Take some time to become aware of your concept of the divine and its place in your life.
- Map out a balanced day, with time allotted for your financial, physical, emotional, and spiritual needs.
- Allow yourself to do nothing for five minutes at least once a day.
- Ask yourself a simple question: How could I spend my days in a way that would make me feel excited about waking up in the morning? The answer may help lead you toward more balance in your life.
- Try this balancing exercise: For the next seven days, keep a diary of your personal and professional time. Notice how much time you devote to each aspect of your life. Then ask yourself if you'd find any adjustments to your time allocation advisable. Are you investing your time in those people, places, and things that you treasure most deeply?
- Don't wait for a huge chunk of free time to materialize before you try these suggestions; find the time where you are now, in the present.

CHAPTER FOUR

THE CONTEMPLATIVE PRACTICE

Man's activity consists in either a making or a doing.
Both of these aspects of the active life depend for
their correction on the contemplative life.

—*A. K. Coomeraswamy*

STEVEN SCHWARTZ IS A STUNNING example of the value of doing nothing. Each morning, as the world begins its daily spiral into frantic activity, he simply sits still. And at the end of the day, with the outside buzz ebbing, he does it again. Two hours of stillness in all. Yet any lawyer would envy the amount he gets done.

Schwartz is the founder and executive director of the Center for Public Representation, a public-interest law firm based in Northampton and Newton, Massachusetts, that predominantly represents mentally disabled clients. His particular version of "being" without "doing" comes from Buddhist meditation tradition.

In 1971, after finishing Harvard Law School, Schwartz traveled in Asia, where he became deeply involved in Vipassana meditation, an ancient technique based on close observation of the breath. Today his formal practice consists of daily morning and evening sittings, total-ing about two hours. That may sound like an absurd amount of time to spend in silence, accomplishing nothing, especially considering the demands of running the Center, which has a ten-lawyer staff, advises groups nationwide on disability law issues, and does a great deal of liti-gation and appellate work. And Schwartz is married and has a young son. But in fact he accomplishes an amazing amount by simply sitting and turning inward.

A Practice That Quiets the Mind

Getting off the mental treadmill on a regular basis is essential. It's a basic human need that keeps you sane and contributes to your overall health and sense of well-being. But it is *how* you quiet your mind, and with what quality of awareness you do it, that really determines its ben-efits. The number of misguided ways you can try to tamp down the turmoil is probably endless. You can steamroll through your days, lost in thought, reacting reflexively to the stimuli you encounter, and then sim-ply rely on sleep to quiet the inner buzz. You may get a lot of work done that way, but you won't learn much about yourself, and you'll certainly miss most of what is beautiful and nourishing within and around you. Alternatively, you can party hard, getting lost in mechanical good cheer and hollow interactions, or numb yourself in a thousand other ways, gaining some respite from the pressures of the day but losing more and more of yourself in the process.

Dozens of better choices for escaping your mind's workaday chatter were explored in the *ABA Journal* during the three years it ran "Out of the Office," a regular column looking at what lawyers do when they are not at work. In those mini-profiles, certain consistencies became appar-ent in the activities they chose, most of which tended to:

- demand so much concentration that they pushed the pressures of law practice right out of consciousness—such activities included rac-ing mountain bikes, hot-air ballooning, rodeo riding, rock climbing, race car driving, and competing in triathlons
- take the lawyers out of "office time" and entrain them to a differ-ent pace or rhythm—such things as gardening, painting, cooking, and bird-watching fulfilled this need

- allow for the possibility of achieving "flow," the state often described by athletes as being "in the zone," and characterized by a sense of effortless grace, even in the midst of a very demanding endeavor— underwater cave diving, surfing, gliding, aerobatic flying, and many of the activities previously listed all offered this possibility

Hobbies are wonderful, and while you are doing them, they often serve to keep the judgmental, demanding wolves at bay. But something more is needed if you want to develop your personal and professional life into one that brings you joy and satisfaction, while also feeding your need for serenity, spiritual connection, and a centered existence. Many have found that meditation addresses all these needs and more.

A huge amount of research has now documented the health benefits of both meditation and prayer, and hospitals all over the country reflect this. Hundreds offer training in meditation, and most seem to provide quiet places for contemplation of whatever kind. In the worlds of education, the arts and sciences, philanthropy, and even now in business, there is a new openness to contemplative avenues of understanding and a realization that these approaches can complement linear thinking and scientific empiricism.

For Schwartz, whose legal work so clearly embodies the fruits of his contemplative life, law practice without the stabilizing and insight-producing influences of meditation would be unthinkable.

Level One: Meditating on a Brief

Meditation enriches his legal work in ways that range from the supremely practical to the somewhat arcane. All of it, though, is of a piece and is central to understanding Schwartz and his commitment to alleviating the suffering of mentally disabled people, which is the Center's primary mission.

Schwartz says that, for him, meditation works on four different levels. The first, which he describes as the most simplistic and mundane, is almost startlingly practical. For the first ten or fifteen minutes of his hour-and-a-half morning sitting, before his mind becomes quiet, he enters what he describes as a space that allows him to think in a highly creative way about his work and, specifically, about problems and obstacles he's likely to face that day. During this period, he outlines and plans briefs, oral arguments, systemic settlement orders, and negotiations; he also plans structural changes for the firm and formulates his to-do list.

"For an oral argument, I will literally outline it in five minutes," he says. "That's how it comes to me." Schwartz says there are two reasons he is able to do this. "First, my mind is not operating in a linear way. It free-associates, so I'm not trapped by the requirement that I begin by thinking of what comes first—which is hard to do when you don't know what else is coming." Second, he says, *he has nothing to do.* "My mind is not engaged in any dialogue with the world, whether it be with my computer, with opposing counsel, or with a client."

Schwartz says he'll come up with about 90 percent of a document's first draft this way, probably 60 percent of the final version. "I just wrote a brief to the U.S. Supreme Court on behalf of a group of disability organizations on whether or not the ADA (Americans With Disabilities Act) applies to prisons," he says. "It raised a lot of constitutional questions. The outline was all in a free space in my consciousness, and then it just settled."

Quick to point out that this does not happen every time he meditates, Schwartz says he never tries to force the process. "It would never dawn on me when I sit down that I'm going to outline a brief. Sometimes it happens on the first day I sit with the problem; sometimes it's on the tenth day." He treasures this ability and feels grateful for it. "It saves me an unbelievable amount of time," he says. "And it is sublimely, precisely correct."

Level Two: Connecting with Compassion

Unlike the first level of benefits—creative thinking and saving time— the second way in which Schwartz's meditation practice enriches his legal work has to do with what he calls a noncognitive function. But it, too, has profound practical implications.

"It is primarily about a personal connection with the compassion and feeling levels that inspire my work," he says. "It might take the form of reflection on a particular client I'm working with or a group of people. It's an emotional connection I have with people, which gets sharpened and refined during the practice." The practical value of this connection, says Schwartz, is this: "It is singularly why I've been able to do the same work for twenty-seven years without being overwhelmed by the pain and my feelings for these devalued people."

The threat of burnout may always be there—as it is for all professionals who deal with the mentally ill—but for Schwartz, the daily inward journey provides sustenance and strength that keeps him going, not by offering escape, but by allowing him to forge a deeper relationship with the people he serves.

Level Three: Boosting Energy

A third, more personal, dimension of meditation for Schwartz is the daily renewal it offers. "The energy and the constancy and the commitment—the determination of mind to do what I do . . . it's a place of reestablishing or reconnecting to the energy and purpose of my work as an attorney. That energy is reestablished every day. When I get up from sitting, I have an enormous amount of energy to do the work. People are amazed at how long I can work without stopping."

The literature on meditation is full of stories about people whose practices drastically boosted their personal energy and actually reduced their need for sleep. It may have something to do with what author and meditation teacher Jack Kornfield refers to as "stopping the war within." Because meditation promotes nonjudgmental observation of one's own body and mind, it gradually makes you aware of the disruptive and divisive role judgment can play in all aspects of your life (separating "me" from "others" or even from "myself," for example). This growing awareness can foster a mental orientation in which the things lawyers tend to automatically view as separate and even contentious—us/them, lawyer/client, client/community—are more easily seen as harmonious parts of a single whole. As Kornfield points out, war is exhausting, and the fact that certain artificial separations have, by consensus, become part of our outer reality doesn't mean you have to be inwardly divided. In helping you to recognize the common ground you share with other people, contemplative practices enable you to go beyond such divisions and release the energies required to sustain them.

Level Four: Moving into Clarity

Finally, Schwartz says, comes the most profound dimension of his contemplative practice. "It's about discerning what is really true in the most fundamental way. It's a question of right understanding. It happens in a lot of ways. I can see the way in which opposing counsel is trying to take advantage or to rattle me, for example. And I can relate pretty quickly to the motive or intention behind their actions. Sometimes it's just nasty, and sometimes it's based on lack of understanding, but this level always allows me the greatest possibility of seeing those things and therefore allows me the most opportunity to communicate and work with it.

"It is also in this space that I realize that the truth of this work is that it is a long haul. For the last two hundred years, the United States has confined people with disabilities in institutions and asylums. If it's taken that long to create the system, it's going to take some time to overhaul it. Realizing this allows me a little distance. It gives me a truer understanding of what it's about."

It is hard to overestimate these benefits for lawyers. Imagine being able to see more deeply into the other side's motives so that actions you might find infuriating suddenly become worthy of understanding or even compassion. From that position, you're more likely to reach a mutually agreeable resolution. Then too, the ability to see your work in a broad and generous context, so that it isn't cramped by the matters heaped before you, can deepen your appreciation of the ultimate significance of your work and your resolve to forge ahead.

Staying on the Beam

It takes great commitment and a certain amount of faith to hew to the rigors of a contemplative practice, and as Schwartz hastens to point out, any one—or none—of the experiences he describes may arise in a given meditation session. But the rewards—clarity, strength, courage, compassion, and an enriching sense of context—have brought extraordinary depth to his life and to his law practice, as has an almost unshakable sense of balance.

"We spend a lot of time negotiating on behalf of clients who want to get out of institutions," Schwartz says. "We're often talking to doctors on the wards or to supervisors. If those talks aren't conducted really skillfully, we won't get our clients out. We've got to be able to appeal to that person's interest in wanting to release our client. But often we don't get what we want. If you lose it in that situation, lose your sense of balance and flip out, you're not helping your clients. You have to have skills of reflection and self-confidence and ways of staying balanced in the face of very difficult and challenging situations.

"I often emphasize that the work can't be about winning. It's got to be about something much more important than that. It's hard for aggressive lawyers to think about perspectives not grounded in winning. But it really has to be about a sense of balance where you can muster all the research skills, the ability to skillfully conduct intense cross-examinations, and so on, but your motive can't be about yourself. It must be about service. If it is, it changes everything. And that's not reserved for people on white horses, people in the public-interest community. I think it applies to all lawyers."

To help all its employees stay connected and feel supported, the Center for Public Representation provides space for quiet contemplation in the office. "There's a real sense here that these things matter," Schwartz says, "that these are valued attitudes." Indeed, what Schwartz refers to as "the work" has a beauty and an integrity to it that is hard to imagine without the powerful influence of contemplative practice. In a very real sense, it makes the work possible, enjoyable, satisfying, and endlessly renewing.

"It's a public-interest law firm that pays nothing," Schwartz says. "By most people's measures, we're not doing very well. But we have a clear sense of purpose and mission." The palpability of that sense of purpose says something profound about the Center for Public Representation: that its people have learned to heal—or at the very least minimize—the split between their institutional and human identities. This should offer great hope to lawyers, whose happiness and effectiveness on a human level depend on it. It has certainly meant a lot to the Center's lawyers, half of whom have been there for twenty years or more.

For their counterparts in corporate law firms, it is becoming increasingly difficult to sustain the energy and commitment to stick around at the same place for twenty or more years. But one lawyer who has done exactly that, at the Boston firm of Bingham Dana LLP, is offering the secret of his longevity and vigor to a group of colleagues who are willing to admit they need it before the stress simply becomes too much.

Corporate Law and Yoga

For an hour and a half on Thursday nights, Justin Morreale creates his own sacred space at Bingham Dana. Morreale has practiced law for two more years than he's practiced yoga—thirty years in the law; twenty-eight at yoga. He is convinced he would never have survived, much less thrived in, the world of high-powered corporate law without his yoga practice.

Today he wears four professional hats. He runs Bingham Dana's 100-lawyer corporate department, sits on the firm's management committee, serves as cochair of Bingham's business development group, and has his own practice, in which he represents such clients as the Boston Red Sox and a variety of emerging companies, mostly in the biomedical and high-tech fields. He is also married and has seven children.

"I have a lot of streams and tributaries coming into me, even if I'm not involved in doing all the deals," he says. "Every day, I get dozens of E-mails and voice mails, people are constantly coming into my office, and I've got lots of board meetings and conferences with clients to attend to.

"What yoga does for me is that it allows me to process the stress in a certain way, a way that makes it all work for me," he says. "Most people in my situation would be wired all the time. I'm not."

As Morreale points out, yoga is fundamentally a contemplative practice. Like meditation, it involves cultivating attention and awareness. In its classical Indian forms, hatha yoga, the physical posture component of the practice, was incidental, mere preparation for sitting meditation practice. And that is how Morreale uses it. Every morning after doing about an hour of yogic postures, he meditates. In the West, however, it is more common for practitioners to focus on the physical part of yoga as the primary practice.

"Hatha yoga has a spiritual, contemplative component to it," Morreale says, "if it is done with an awareness, and with concentration on the breath. It's as if you use the body to capture the mind, so that the mind is no longer shopping, or thinking about the Red Sox game. When you bring the mind into the body this way, it's not just good for your body, but you also end up leaving behind the E-mails and conference calls."

Morreale had an interest in what he calls nontraditional practices even before he discovered yoga, so that when he was introduced to the practice, there was what he calls "some spiritual pull." That is not necessarily the case with the students in the yoga class he now teaches once a week at Bingham Dana. Most of them come simply to relax and learn ways to manage the stresses that buffet them throughout the week.

"This is so powerful for lawyers who have been hanging out in the left side of their brains for so long," Morreale says. "I try to get them to be with their bodies and their breath, and to do an easygoing meditation at the end. They just die for that. They tell me they hadn't thought it was possible to be in this building and feel this good."

Simple Yogic Breathing ———————————————

Yogic breathing can be done anytime you have a few spare minutes and a little privacy. Some techniques, such as the one commonly known as "breath of fire," have an energizing effect. Others, including the type described here—the "sweet breath"—are particularly relaxing, although they have an energizing component as well. For people who practice hatha yoga, doing yogic breathing during the day is a way of bringing back the deep relaxation that the postures inspire. But even without the formal practice to call on, nonpractitioners can benefit from the techniques' profoundly relaxing effects.

Instructions for Nadi Shoshanna ("Sweet Breath")

First, curl your index finger and middle finger into the palm of your right hand. You will use your thumb to close your right nostril, and your ring finger and little finger together to close off your left nostril.

Step 1: Close the right nostril with your thumb, then gently exhale and then inhale through the left nostril.
Step 2: Close the left nostril, and exhale and inhale through the right nostril. Steps 1 and 2 complete one round.
Step 3: Repeat, alternating nostrils after each inhalation.

Make sure your breathing is deep, full, and relaxed. Do not strain. Do not hold your breath. If at first the breath is uneven, that's OK. After a few minutes it will settle into a natural rhythm. Don't count or control the breath. Just let go and enjoy yourself.

Morreale is constantly amazed at how consistently yoga helps people, even in very immediate ways, to overcome stress. Although he doesn't really know how it works on the physiological, chemical, or spiritual levels, he says it works for almost everyone. As evidence, he tells how learning yogic breathing changed the life of one lawyer who works at very high stress levels, running around town from client to client, crisis to crisis. As a result of taking Morreale's class, he now routinely pulls off the road in the afternoon to do a couple minutes of yogic breathing. "He says it changes his day and has changed his life in ways that go beyond his work," Morreale explains.

In his classes, Morreale incorporates clinical evidence about the benefits of yoga, but he says his students really don't need it. They love the way it feels, and once they've started doing yoga, they seem to understand intuitively that there is something in it that they need. "I see lawyers acting in ways they probably haven't since kindergarten," he says, referring to the energy and spontaneity they demonstrate in class.

One student—business lawyer Leslie Shapiro, whose legal career has encompassed government work, teaching, and most other things you can do in the law—has found the benefits of Morreale's class to be profound and practical. "Not long ago, I got caught at the Newark airport. After an eleven-hour day, I ran like a lunatic to catch my plane, because I had to get back to Boston for a commitment," she recalls. "Once I got on the plane, we sat on the runway for an hour and a half in what felt like 112-degree heat. I was not happy.

"But I found myself thinking, 'Breathe, breathe, just breathe.' And I did one of the techniques Justin had taught us, and it really worked. I now have this tool that I didn't have before for dealing with the stress."

Shapiro says it wasn't the spiritual side of yoga that attracted her to the class; it was the stress reduction. "But I figure anything that has lasted as long as yoga has been around has definitely got something to it, and I respect a lot of the basic wisdom inherent in it—the idea of listening to the body, keeping the right perspective, not getting too caught up in the moment and losing sight of the larger world, and so on. And I think that anything that reduces the stress people are under and helps them behave more constructively, sanely, and creatively is a good thing. Yoga is definitely good for lawyers."

For Morreale, the question of whether or not to practice yoga or some other contemplative practice is, to use the vernacular, a no-brainer. "It enhances everything in life," he says, "relationships, work, and any wisdom tradition that is already there for you. You start to see more clearly, you become more open, and you understand and appreciate more. A teacher of mine used to say that everything comes through the same door. If you're not open, you don't get the pain, but you also don't get the love, the beauty, the joy. A real key to lawyering is making sure that other lawyers and clients have an easy time relating to you. It's what rainmaking is all about too. If people feel you're open and you can hear them—if they sense you have some inner depth—they tend to be drawn to you and trust you more."

THE GREEN GROUP GOES CONTEMPLATIVE

The spiritual benefits of contemplative practices have been known for thousands of years. And in recent decades, their profound health benefits have been studied and documented. Another facet of their power, however, is only just starting to be understood and applied in our society: their ability to enrich communication, heal rifts, and unite people on a deep level to pursue a common goal.

This is something the Green Group has come to appreciate. The Group is composed of CEOs of major national environmental organizations such as the Sierra Club, National Resources Defense Council, and the Wilderness Society. Most Group members are male, most are rather aggressive, and most are lawyers. And when it comes to building bridges and finding commonality on a deep level, most face the same tendencies and obstacles that plague their colleagues who work in law offices.

Not long ago, Green Group members realized that they faced a conundrum. Evidence showed that churches and synagogues were playing the most significant role in raising the public's environmental awareness, bringing into question the continuing relevance of the organizations that the Green Group represents.

The Group wisely decided to figure out why these religious bodies had enjoyed such efficacy in communicating the vital importance of conservancy to their flocks. In other words, they decided to learn more about the sacred roots of environmental responsibility across faiths. To do this, they approached Paul Gorman at New York's Cathedral of St. John the Divine, who heads the National Religious Partnership for the Environment. Gorman suggested that the Group try coming together in a contemplative way, to spend some time together in silence—and only then talk about their concerns.

Group members had never been particularly close. They met principally because they had goals in common but tended to be turf conscious and competitive, their relationships fraught with internal friction. So when Mirabai Bush of the Center for Contemplative Mind in Society— which develops and promotes contemplative practice through courses like the one at Yale Law School (see Chapter 12)—was asked to run a retreat for the Group, she was clear about the challenges she would face. "These are not tree-hugger types," she says. "They are definitely CEO types."

And so the Group convened at a retreat center far from Washington and New York, where nearly all of the members are based. There, they were taught both walking and sitting meditation, and they spent the greater part of each day in silence, speaking only at specified times.

According to Phillip Clapp of the National Environmental Trust, the retreat was an extraordinary success. "The kinds of relationships our market economy tends to create as a substitute for other kinds . . . we don't relate to each other as people, but as institutions and roles. That's how it had been in the Group."

What changed that, says Clapp, who has meditated for years, was the silence. It helped members distance themselves from their institutional identities and remember why they wanted to be heads of environmental groups in the first place—a vision they often lost in the pressure to raise money or to be *the* group that is most expert on a given issue. In Clapp's view, there is no question that the retreat created an ability to communicate on a human level that had not been there before. "We really realized that the more cooperatively we work together, the better the movement will be," he says. "Of course, you have to do it more than once, and we are committed to continuing it. It's interesting, because they are definitely not a spiritually oriented group."

They are, however, results oriented, and not only did a new sense of cohesion arise as a result of the first retreat, but so did several concrete goals. Together with the Center for Contemplative Practice and the Partnership for the Environment, the Green Group formalized these goals:

- Facilitate greater collaboration among national environmental organizations by providing an opportunity in a contemplative environment for Green Group CEOs to know one another (and themselves) beyond institutional personas and agendas.
- Draw out and explore religious, spiritual, and moral perspectives generally unspoken within the environmental movement.
- Provide a foundation of understanding and trust between secular environmental organizations and the American religious community.

After the Group's first retreat, they worked together on the Clean Air Act, which was coming up for reauthorization. They now attribute their success in that effort to having been together in such an open way at the retreat, and to bringing that spirit of openness into discussions about what they see as their common work in the twenty-first century.

For Clapp, it shows that when people have a passionate commitment to a common goal, only their socially constructed roles stand in their way. "When they start relating to each other on the basis that they share a complete and total commitment with each other, when they realize they have a prime directive, there's no limit to what they can accomplish."

TRANSFORMING YOUR PRACTICE

For centuries, and in cultures all over the world, a contemplative practice of some kind has been considered basic, one of life's essential ingredients. Such practices provide a dependable and gradual opening to the inner life and the riches it holds. Lawyers who regularly meditate, pray, practice yoga, or spend quiet time in nature or in some similar practice find that it helps them see the world afresh. The events of the day touch them at a level that makes their meaning clearer (this may include legal meaning but is by no means limited to that). New kinds of solutions emerge for familiar problems, and the interpersonal aspect of lawyering becomes both more compelling and much more rewarding.

The first step to implementing a contemplative practice is to make a commitment to giving it a try. Commit to a month, at the end of which you can assess its value to you. The least that will happen is you'll get a daily break from the grind. In most cases, though, you'll find that the time spent in contemplation is richly rewarded by its effects on the rest of your day.

Here are a few additional tips:

• Spend a little time learning about what practices are available, what each requires in terms of time commitment, equipment (mats or cushions, for example), and training. Public libraries and bookstores are full of books on spiritual practice, so have a look. Don't rush, though; try to see your "research" as the first step of a journey into yourself.
• Choose the practice that feels right to you, the one with the emphasis and texture (for lack of a better word) that speak to you. Do you prefer something with a physical component, something that might help you get out of your head? Would you rather do

Two Meditation Exercises

Basic Sitting Meditation

To prepare, simply sit comfortably, either on the floor or in a chair. If you sit on the floor, place a cushion under your buttocks to raise your hips. If you are not sitting on carpet, you should use padding of some sort to keep your knees and ankles comfortable. Sit cross-legged, kneeling, or in a half-lotus or full-lotus position, whatever is most comfortable for you. If you sit in a chair, move forward slightly from the back. Wherever you choose to sit, relax into your seat, but maintain a dignified position, with your spine straight but not stiff.

Step 1: Softly close your eyes.

Step 2: Take a few deep breaths, paying special attention to where the sensation of breathing is clearest to you. Usually, this will be either at the nostrils, in the rise and fall of the abdomen, or in the chest.

Step 3: Having chosen a place to observe the breath, breathe naturally, without forcing anything. Become aware of your breath as it enters your body and as it leaves. Watch it closely, noticing the *sensations* as they come and go, observing them in a spirit of exploration.

Step 4: When thoughts come to your mind—and they will, frequently—simply notice them and then return your focus to the breath.

Step 5: Keep your concentration on the breath, and notice whatever comes up in your awareness. Try to be accepting of yourself regardless of what arises. Meditation is about being fully yourself in the moment, not about any external measure of correctness. Return to the breath as often as necessary.

Step 6: Notice that your awareness is larger than your thoughts and can contain your thoughts. Rest comfortably in this spacious awareness—just breathing, just noticing. Try sitting for ten minutes. When you are comfortable with that, try extending it to twenty minutes.

Window Meditation

This meditation can be practiced in any law office with a window. Describing the effect of the practice, one meditation teacher said it's like "pushing the clear button on your mental calculator."

Begin by standing in front of a window in the "mountain pose." To do this, stand with your feet a hip's width apart, then become aware of their being connected firmly to the floor. Move your attention up through your body to the very top of your head. Then, feel the top of the head being drawn up toward the sky. The idea here is to embody the dignity of a mountain, being at once firmly grounded, erect, and *present*.

Then open your awareness to just seeing, realizing that seeing and looking are not the same thing. *Looking* implies a directed intention; *seeing* means opening to whatever presents itself in your visual awareness.

First, develop a one-pointed focus by choosing something in particular to watch. It can be a person walking, a cloud, a moving car, or a tree. The important thing is to keep your awareness focused on seeing just that one thing.

Next, experiment with opening your awareness and taking in the whole scene as everything in that scene comes and goes. Think of it as maintaining a panoramic attention.

Every time your mind moves to something else, starts making up stories about what you're seeing, or begins to think about the rest of your day, gently come back to just seeing.

When you decide to stop, bring your attention back to your body, and become aware of your breath in the body. Then take a couple of big, intentional breaths before moving into the next activity of your day. And remember: it's not the length of time you devote to this practice that matters; it's the quality of presence you bring to it.

(With thanks to Ferris B. Urbanowski of the Stress Reduction Clinic at the University of Massachusetts Medical Center.)

---

it alone, or would you be more comfortable with something that allows for group practice—say, at a church or synagogue, a mosque or a meditation center?

- Try to find people who will talk about their practices with you, especially colleagues—that is, if you know someone who feels comfortable doing so. It'll give you a better sense of how such a practice can mesh with and enhance a law practice.
- Start slow. Whatever practice you decide to try, take it a little bit at a time. Don't expect too much of yourself; or, if you do, don't get down on yourself for that. Allow it and let it pass. Being "good"

at it is emphatically not the point. Let your practice be a vacation from having to succeed, please others, or do things "right." Instead, make it a time to just be: to be yourself, as you are in the moment, in your body, awake.

• Keep in mind that although your experience on the path you begin will be uniquely yours, there are dips and curves that you may (or may not) encounter. If you do, be aware that others have been there too. If you feel frustrated or confused, remember that there are plenty of guides to dealing with any obstacles that may arise. So find out about the resources in your area for the practice you've chosen. Know who the respected teachers and advisers are, and familiarize yourself with books known for their clarity about how to stay on the path.

CHAPTER FIVE

THE MINDFUL PRACTICE

Only that day dawns to which we are awake.
—*Henry David Thoreau*

Actio sequitur esse: Action follows being.

HERE ARE SOME OF THE THINGS that Florida plaintiff's attorney Warren Anderson tries to be mindful of while he's working on a case:

- the essential beauty of life, and the fact that handling this particular case is why he went to law school
- that accepting representation of another human being is a serious commitment and should always be treated as such
- that it is important to always try to see the situation from the other side's point of view
- that both the case and his clients "interconnect with the larger web of life"
- that the situation calls for humbleness, restraint, and compassion even while he is zealously representing his client within the law

59

But his mindfulness doesn't stop there. He tries to be wholly present to whatever he is doing, thinking, and feeling. That is the essence of mindfulness, as it has been practiced—mostly in the East—for thousands of years.

Realizing that he, like the rest of us, habitually gets lost in thoughts, expectations, and automatic emotional reactions, Anderson acknowledges that the practice is a challenge. "It's a couple-step process. I often catch myself not doing it, and then I try to do it. The thing is, we're trained not to do it and to just represent clients zealously at the expense of everything else. But it's a practice that helps me remember that I have a responsibility to more than just that—to the court, to justice, to ethics."

As an example of how he tries and sometimes fails to practice mindfulness, Anderson, whose office is in Jacksonville Beach, describes an incident in which he wrote a letter to a lawyer in Ohio who was acting as local counsel for one of his clients in that state. Because it was a health-related matter, Anderson summarized his client's physical condition, including various preexisting problems. "I would have been thrilled with that if I were him," he says. "But then I dictated interrogatories for him too. So I did the lion's share of the work, while he'll get the lion's share of the fee.

"Now, he didn't ask me to do all this work, but I wrote him a letter and I said, essentially, from now on, you'll do all the work. It was fairly cold. Well, my paralegal saw the letter and pointed out to me that the tone was not exactly gracious. So I changed it. Instead of saying, 'Step up to the plate; you're getting paid for this!' I wrote, 'I hope the material helps. Let me know if we can be of further assistance.' I had not been practicing mindfulness, and it required that she point out to me how a little phrase could be taken, how it could affect someone else. Some time ago, she spent a week with Jon Kabat-Zinn, and so she's predisposed to help me with certain things, like my tendency to get disappointed with people and lose perspective."

HOW MINDFULNESS HELPS

At the Stress Reduction Clinic at the University of Massachusetts Medical Center, Jon Kabat-Zinn has been demonstrating over the past twenty years how practicing mindfulness can reduce stress and enhance health and well-being. In fact, researchers recently documented that the part of the brain responsible for generating positive feelings becomes significantly more active as a result of undergoing the type of training Kabat-Zinn has pioneered. Although the roots of mindfulness practice are in Buddhism, Kabat-Zinn's achievement has been to bring it to mainstream Western institutions, including business, health care, education, and, most recently, law.

He describes mindfulness, which is more easily experienced than put into words, as paying attention in a particular way: on purpose, in the present moment, and nonjudgmentally. It's a kind of meditation, done standing up or sitting down, at home, at work, in the car—anywhere and everywhere. It is simple but far from easy, and its effects can be powerful and transformative, which is why courses modeled after the UMass program have sprung up throughout the country.

What makes the practice of mindfulness so valuable for lawyers is that it requires no special equipment and can be done anywhere, at any time. In other words, it is a practice for developing the inner life that can be done *while you practice law.* And it has tremendous practical benefits. When you are mindful of the moment in a nonjudgmental and open way, you can suddenly see things you never noticed before; new choices become possible. You can see stressful situations with greater clarity and calm; this gives you a chance not to lose your balance, and to face the situations creatively and with confidence. No longer on autopilot, you can really look at what is important to you and realize that, although much of what happens to you is beyond your control, you have enormous power over how you respond to, and deal with, whatever comes your way.

In the context of a law practice, these are some of the additional benefits mindfulness offers:

- It can help you become aware of your own biases and prejudices and how they get in the way of effective work.
- It can help you see the potential in difficult moments, so that rather than reacting mindlessly to what is happening on the surface, you have an opportunity to learn what may be going on at a deeper level.
- It can help you become aware of the quality of your own presence—including what you are saying and how you are saying it—so that others' responses become more understandable.

Stacey is a Colorado lawyer who does mostly bankruptcy work. She's had a bit of training in mindfulness and does a fair amount of reading on the subject. When she is mindful, she says, she feels as if she has a whole new palette of options available to her every minute of her day. Suddenly she realizes that this amazing spectrum of choices has been there all along; she had only to turn on the light of awareness to notice it.

When Stacey is practicing mindfully and a colleague or opponent flies off the handle, she tries to simply notice the feelings that come up for her without responding reflexively. Instead, she waits until she's ready. Oftentimes she chooses to look more deeply, to consider what might be behind the outburst. Maybe there's an illness in the person's family, or perhaps someone just told him off.

In the past, when an interview with a client was getting off track, Stacey became self-critical; internal voices told her she really didn't know what she was doing and even questioned her choice of work. Now when that happens, she just watches it happening, often noticing that her stomach is knotting up. She lets herself be aware of it all without having to get attached to it. She doesn't fight the voices or the physical sensations, so they have no real power over her. Suddenly she becomes aware that she can choose to work with the client in a different way. She stops, takes a mindful breath, and thinks about how she might connect with the person in her office in a way that helps them both find their way.

As a rule, lawyers do not consider the value of their own inner resources, those that exist in their bodies and minds. Practicing mindfulness gives you a chance to explore them.

"We do and do and do, but we don't stop to reflect on who's doing the doing," Kabat-Zinn has written. "We feel cut off from our own experience and feelings. We are driven by the mind, by thought, by expectations, by fear, by wanting to get somewhere else. If you always want to be someplace else, then you are never actually where you are, and therefore not fully alive. Nor are you capable of dealing with the pressures and difficulties that arise if your mind is inattentive and is half not here. . . . The deeper levels of intelligence and wisdom that come from clear and full seeing will not be available to you because of this foggy cloud in the mind."

When you are mindful, you notice that it isn't just your mind that is engaged in your work; it's also your body and your heart. Everything you *do* has a correlate on the level of being—it is felt and understood in an inner way. Being aware of that inner experience can make life—and work—much more interesting and much more enjoyable.

BEING WITH THE BREATH

In mindfulness practice, the primary tool for cutting through the fog in the mind and finding your place in the present moment is awareness of your breath. As a focus for attention, it is unsurpassed. It's always there with you, and it is intimately tied to your presence here on earth, so paying attention to it is an excellent way to remind yourself that you are, in fact, here. *Now.*

If you try staying with a full breath—through inhalation and exhalation—being fully present to how it feels in this moment to just breathe naturally and know that you're breathing, you'll notice that it brings you to an awareness of your body. And the crucial thing about your body is that it knows *only* the moment; it's your mind that takes you into tomorrow when you're actually sitting here, on the phone with a client; or into the past, when you're working on a memorandum against a tight deadline. So awareness of the breath acts as an anchor to bring you back to yourself. In the moment.

And when you try to simply breathe with awareness, the challenge of being present becomes clear. Are you wondering whether you're doing it right? Worrying that you might be wasting your time? Doubting that it has any relevance to your life? These thoughts are perfectly normal, and if you just observe them without judging, they will, like all other thoughts and feelings, dissipate as new mental formations take their place. When you're alive to the present moment, you can see this happen and allow it, and come to realize that all moments are rich with possibilities. It's odd really; the logic behind being where you are is so staggeringly obvious that we tend to overlook it: since you'll never live anywhere else *but* in this moment, in this *now*, why not really be here?

Carlton is a public defender in the Northwest. When he's in trial and it's time to start his cross-examination, he makes a point of connecting with his breath. Inevitably that brings with it a realization that he is in the courtroom representing another human being, not off in his mind somewhere. Then all sorts of things can happen. It's almost as if he can see spaces between moments, enabling him to use each one consciously.

If he is in command of all his materials, if he knows the case inside out, the added sense of self-awareness makes everything flow smoothly and he feels absolutely in control, like a real maestro.

If you can imagine that your awareness is like the sky, in which thoughts and feelings come and go like clouds, then you can choose when it is appropriate to act on any one of them, or simply to watch them drift by. In practical terms, if, in the course of your legal work, the thought "He's trying to get me" crosses your mind and triggers certain impulses, you can do any of several things. You can simply react to the impulses, possibly embarking on a course of action you will come to regret (although you may never know how unnecessary and inappropriate it was). Or, you can step back and realize that—as the sky—your awareness can hold the clouds (i.e., the thought and the impulse) and examine them. Because the sky *contains* the clouds, it needn't be controlled by them. Seeing this, you can then choose to respond or not to respond, depending on what you really want and your now clearer sense of the actual situation.

Paying attention in this way reveals every moment to be fertile and full of potential. "In every moment, things can go a lot of different ways," Kabat-Zinn says, "and we have some say in which way they go, because we can respond instead of just reacting." It is worth noting too that at the other end of the awareness spectrum—the mind*less* end—are the states of mind that quite often underlie lawyer disciplinary actions, whether they have to do with neglecting to return phone calls or forgetting to communicate key information. It needn't happen. With the breath as your anchor and a commitment to being awake and present, awareness *in the moment* is always within reach.

Enhancing Balance

Mindfulness practice not only leads to a greater sense of self-mastery, well-being, and relaxation—a tremendous boon to the tedious juggling of obligations and crises—but it also deepens the ability to concentrate and, over time, says Kabat-Zinn, leads to an experience of interconnectedness "as the fundamental ground of being."

Integrating such awareness into your law practice can help to redress previously hidden imbalances. When you pay attention to your thoughts, feelings, and physical sensations—again, moment to moment and without judgment—you can actually *see* how fragmented you may be in a given moment, how your mind, with its reflexively analytical/dualistic bent, can unwittingly shield you from truths and possibilities that don't fit neatly into any of the prefabricated boxes you carry around. You also become aware of the constant chatter that fills your head—a characteristic not just of lawyers, but, to some degree, of all human beings—and how merely noticing it makes it easier to get past it to what really matters at the moment.

Warren Anderson offers another example, this one of how he *was* mindful of his possible effect on another person at a crucial moment. He was filing a medical malpractice suit against a local ophthalmologist in the small community outside of Jacksonville where he lives. "This guy's an old-timer," Anderson says, "but he did something that cost a forty-year-old woman her eye."

When the complaint was ready to be served, Anderson paused to consider the best way to get it to the doctor. He decided not to give it to the process server, because he knew that being served, either alone or in front of staff and patients, would be painful. To avoid ruining the doctor's day, Anderson arranged to send the papers to his lawyer instead.

It may sound like a small and obvious thing to do, but it's amazing how often the obvious is obscured by our nonpresence in the moment. That's exactly why Anderson finds it so helpful to integrate mindfulness into his law practice. "Sometimes, for example, I don't do so well when people disappoint me," he says. "I get frustrated with incompetence or slowness, and I have to be real careful with that. Also, when clients call me and start whining, I try to get by that and really see what's going on with them. It's so easy to turn them off, but mindfulness practice has helped me stay with them. As a consequence, I get the sense that people really feel like I am there with them. They know I'm giving priority to their case. And it goes beyond just being a nice guy. Some of the webs that connect us all are pretty intricate. It's a matter of paying attention, because what you say to people can be so devastating or cause the wrong reaction, and then they take that reaction into their dealings with others, with family and friends and colleagues and all the rest.

"It comes back to my favorite quote from Thoreau," Anderson says. "He said, 'To affect the quality of the day, that is the highest of arts.' It's true. It's better than being a musician or a sculptor. We all know people who are fully alive, smiling, and grateful almost anytime we see them—

people who don't dwell on gossip, on the negative, but on the beauty, the wonder, the awe of life. I think to live and move through life like that *is* the highest of arts. And I think that bringing mindfulness to your life brings you closer to that."

Non-Doing, Not Knowing

Because of their power to subvert characteristically lawyerlike thinking, two concepts that are central to mindful living can be especially transformative for attorneys. These are the concepts of "non-doing" and "not knowing."

Non-doing, as Kabat-Zinn puts it, is simply letting things be, and allowing them to unfold in their own way. Sitting meditation, discussed in Chapter 4, is the prototypical method of practicing non-doing (and it certainly enhances any kind of mindfulness practice). By dwelling in stillness and simply watching whatever comes into awareness and letting it go where it will, you tap into something deeper than the ephemera of thought.

If you're a lawyer, chances are your external life—the talking, the negotiating, the arguing, the writing, the earning—tends to capture nearly all your attention. It's where you work and live. Or so it seems. The truth is, you also live at a deeper, inner place, where each of these activities also finds expression in a kind of knowing that you must stop occasionally to tap into. This is where your sense of the *meaning* of your work can be found, where your intuitions count, and where you can see the beauty and elegance in each matter before you, as well as in the wholeness of the greater enterprise. This is the realm of non-doing.

The importance of non-doing was central to the work that Kabat-Zinn's colleague, George Mumford, did with the Chicago Bulls. Then-coach Phil Jackson was a long-time student of meditation and thought that Kabat-Zinn's approach might add a new dimension to the team's game. Mumford trained the team in mindfulness over the last four years of their championship reign in the NBA. What Jackson and Mumford tried to convey to the team—and it apparently sank in—was that, in Kabat-Zinn's words, the real importance of meditation and mindfulness is "to let the doing come out of the non-doing. So, from that point of view, we're not saying that the Chicago Bulls don't want to win, but that they're coming from a place that's beyond the kind of dime-store approach to winning that you usually run into." The same is true, he notes, for any kind of performer. When one's doing comes out of an inner stillness, it has a quality to it that the competition can't match. Psychotherapist and author Eric Maisel obviously had the same idea in mind when he wrote that "A wild person with a calm mind can create anything."

As for not knowing, well, it gets tiring having to know everything all the time. It is also counterproductive to even try. It's not that you should advertise the gaps in your knowledge to colleagues or clients—that would certainly show mind*less*ness about the realities of law practice. But you can, at times when it feels right for you, allow yourself the benefit of not knowing, perhaps especially in the early stages of developing a case, when too much certainty could inhibit creative thinking and drastically reduce the number of approaches you might explore.

You've got to be mindful to do this, because you have to consciously *allow* yourself not to know, to create the space in your world for things to surprise you, for answers to come from places you would never have expected, for strange new ideas to arise in your mind without the need to cling to certainties that would, apparently, negate such novel notions.

The business writer Alan Briskin, in a passage from *The Stirring of Soul in the Workplace*, makes the connection between mindfulness and not knowing quite clear: "Suspending certainty," he writes, "is not simply about our ability to look at an idea in new ways; it is the discipline of looking at ourselves having an idea." Doing so, Briskin writes, is to realize that you are "the interpreter and the artist at the boundary of the internal world" which you feel, and the external world with which you interact. It is also to understand that you can choose to let the separation between inner and outer dissolve. Put another way, to live in a state of unexamined certainty and to cling to it *as if it were you*—rather than simply a formation in the embracing sky of your awareness—is to slam shut the door between the inner and outer worlds.

Not knowing is a skill that Clarissa, a family law specialist in Chicago, has found both challenging and ultimately rewarding. She tried it at first in short bursts and in situations that weren't terribly loaded. She did it with her son, for example, when he asked for permission to do something. Instead of leaping to an answer before he'd even finished asking the question, she let herself *not* know how she felt about what he was asking or, for that matter, *not* decide she even knew *what* he was asking until he'd finished asking it. Then, when he did finish, she realized that she had really been involved with *him* rather than with her own thoughts. And she felt good about that.

For Clarissa, who came to understand that getting comfortable with not knowing can actually lead to deeper kinds of knowing, the implications for her law practice were obvious. Particularly in family law, where emotions often run high and off-the-shelf solutions don't always do the trick, allowing room for meaning to emerge without forcing it can be tremendously helpful. Clarissa knew that, in her line of work, to be cut off from your heart and soul and intuition and just grab at the first thing that comes to mind can be very problematic. Developing the inner skills to avoid falling into that trap was, for her, transformative.

A Day in the Mindful Life

Mindfulness can be practiced anytime, from the moment you wake up in the morning until you slip off to sleep at night. Ideally, mindful awareness should be there in every wakeful moment of the day. In fact, it is the very continuity of awareness—from sensation to thought to feeling, across the transitions that fill our days—that makes it so powerful.

Noting, for example, that as you wake up, the first tendency of your emerging consciousness is to clamp down, banishing the sluggish, dream-inflected world of sleep, you may choose to relax and soften the transition into full wakefulness, letting yourself come alive to the day more slowly and naturally.

You may, as you sit up and hang your legs over the bedside, become aware of tension in your back, a feeling that intensifies as thoughts of a ten o'clock deposition arise in your mind. Taking a deep breath, breathing into the tension, you let it go, place your feet on the floor, and stand up.

Remaining mindful of your surroundings, you hear the bedsheets rustle and turn to gaze at your spouse, whose eyes are open, looking your way. When you smile at each other, you are aware of a sense of gratitude.

The next thing you know, you are in the shower, soaping yourself, wondering how you got there. You realize your mindfulness lapsed for a time and left you lost in anxious thoughts about the depo and a meeting this afternoon with the CEO of a high-tech start-up whom you would love to have as a client. But you don't have to dwell on the lapse—it is natural, part of the process, not worth foundering on.

You remain mindful as best you can, maintaining awareness up to and after the lapses, occasionally noticing things that lift your heart—your daughter's latest drawing on the refrigerator, the sun through an opening in the living room curtains. You make a special point of keeping your awareness as you say goodbye to the family, giving hugs and kisses, making eye contact, letting them matter to you as much as they really do. . . .

Later, at the deposition, things are going reasonably well. At one point, you find familiar thoughts arising in your mind, some of them about the other side's lawyer. "He's doing this just to stick it to me," is one. "Arrogant bastard!" is another. But you let them pass, knowing that you want only to act intentionally, not automatically, mindlessly. And so the moment passes and new moments arise, and in each one you see that you have choices—to speak or not to speak, to interpret a response generously or with skepticism or even scorn, to embody integrity or a lack of it. By the time the deposition is over, you feel unusually satisfied, pleased to have seen and heard, felt and appreciated as much as you did. You feel a renewed strength to take on the rest of the day.

USING MINDFULNESS TO REUNITE WORK AND LIFE

A few years ago, after taking an eight-week course based on Jon Kabat-Zinn's book *Full Catastrophe Living* at a local hospital, Susan, a San Francisco litigator, was interested in carrying on and deepening her mindfulness practice. One of the teachers in the course was a student at the Nyingma Institute in Berkeley, and she suggested that Susan try taking a course there.

The Institute, which was founded in 1972 by the Tibetan Buddhist teacher Tarthang Tulku, had by then played a significant role in the lives of thousands of California lawyers. Its one-day stress-reduction course for lawyers, based on a series of exercises drawn from Tulku's training in Tibetan medicine and yoga, was one of the first in the state to be approved for continuing legal education credit and is offered at sites throughout the Bay Area and in Southern California.

Even today, CLE gets lawyers through the door, but something else accounts for the large number who come back. On questionnaires handed out after the course, 95 percent of attendees say they would recommend the course to a friend or colleague. Many say they think it should be mandatory for attorneys. "Some of the insights and some of the things communicated during the day really stay with people," says Ralph McFall, codirector of the Institute.

Tulku founded Nyingma with the intention of creating a forum for bringing the practices and concepts that he thought applicable from his Tibetan training into Western society. Having spent his first years in the United States becoming acquainted with the country and what he believed to be its needs, he was struck by the amount of tension caused by the speed with which we live our lives. Unfortunately, he observed, the intellectual training we get—although invaluable—tends to cut us off from the body and the senses. He offered tools to redress this imbalance.

"Although for some people, talk of the mind-body connection sounds rather abstract, it actually makes a lot of difference in our lives," says McFall. "When you're under a lot of stress, you don't see things— you don't see pretty flowers, for example, as you walk down the street. Your visual sense is constricted. The same thing happens when you eat food and your sensation of taste becomes flattened. Everything is dulled when you're under stress. The way Tarthang Tulku explains this is to say that the mind and the body aren't talking to each other."

McFall recalls that, on many occasions, after completing an exercise in the stress-reduction course, a lawyer would ask him whether the lights in the room had suddenly been turned up. "What had happened is that they had just hit a spot where their minds and bodies had started communicating again. When that happens, things take on a certain vividness. Colors deepen, and sounds seem more melodious."

The second thing that struck Tulku early on in his life in the United States was how common it was for people to be dissatisfied with their work, devoting long hours to it without experiencing any pleasure, meaning, or sense of intrinsic value. He noticed that people often believe work is to be done in order to get something else—a comfortable retirement, perhaps, or a vacation or a boat—resulting in a perceived division between work and "life."

His solution to the problem—which he laid out in his book *Skillful Means*—is to look at work as a kind of self-training that blends the spiritual and the practical. What is necessary, Tulku maintains, is that we see the work value of getting a good result as simultaneously being a way to grow as human beings. Work should be not only about achievement, in the sense of getting the job done and doing it well, but also an opportunity to develop integrity, honesty, loyalty, responsibility, and cooperation.

Consider the process of making widgets. Let's say you make twenty a day, motivated by the notion that widgets are valuable. But suppose you decide to try to make more. First, you study the process of widget making. After all, you want to make a good product. But then, while you're working, you study your mind in the process of working. You train your mind in concentration, looking at what works and what doesn't. As you make the widgets, you begin to learn about yourself—what distracts you, what helps you focus, how your mind works. Suddenly you've made thirty widgets, but you've also got the bonus of understanding yourself and your mind better.

Tulku refers to this kind of mindfulness practice as "skillful means." It focuses specifically on work, so that it can come to be seen as an integral part of—rather than separate from—the rest of life, a place where all the same thoughts, sensations, and feelings pertain. According to McFall, Tulku's approach to living a more enlightened life puts work at its very center. "He believes it's easier to fool yourself about whether you're developing for the better when you're sitting on a meditation cushion than if you're making a payroll. It should play out in the practical realm."

Tulku himself presents good evidence for this. He arrived in the United States in 1969, totally unacquainted with Western culture. Today he is founder and director of two publishing companies, the Nyingma Institute, and a retreat center.

Mindfulness and the Law

Susan, the San Francisco litigator who took the mindfulness course inspired by Kabat-Zinn's work, had a subsequent personal breakthrough during a one-week summer retreat. "For work practice, I was cutting chevrons, the little fingers that fly independently at the end of Tibetan prayer flags," she recalls. "It isn't easy work. I cut twelve the first day and twenty-four the second day. By the time I got to the fourth day, I was really concentrating. I was tense, my shoulders were up—the way I thought you're supposed to be when you're working hard."

The next day, her teacher told her to work on enjoying what she was doing—enjoy the color and the feeling of the fabric, and, because she was working indoors and the windows were open, enjoy the breeze on her skin. "Well," she recalls, "my answer to that was, 'You've got to be kidding. Can I assume no one will get mad at me if I cut only five chevrons?'

 Exercise: Mindful Walking/Walking Meditation

It is possible to bring mindfulness to anything you do. One activity that lends itself particularly well to mindfulness is walking, since we do it so often and there are so many physical sensations involved in the activity. Here are two approaches to bringing mindfulness to walking:

Casual Walking Practice

Step 1:   Decide where you're going to walk. Make sure it won't involve too many starts and stops, and that you won't have to walk through traffic or anything else that demands much attention. Try walking around the block for starters.

Step 2:   Begin walking, focusing all your attention on what you are doing. Depending on your speed, you can bring your attention either to each movement of the feet or legs—lifting, moving, placing, for example—or to the body as a whole. In either case, the goal is to *be* walking, noticing every sensation you can *as they arise*.

Step 3:   When you find yourself drifting away from your focus, into thought or resistance of any kind, simply notice where your mind has gone, and return to the sensations in your feet, legs, or entire body.

Formal Walking Meditation

The instructions are essentially the same as for Casual Walking, only the practice is done in a place where there are no external distractions—no need to walk around other people, be aware of streetlights, and so forth. You might try it, for example, in your office, your living room, or your backyard, as long as you can walk in a straight line for at least fifteen steps before turning around and walking back again. Walk back and forth *slowly* with complete awareness for ten minutes.

"I ended up doing four times as many as I'd done before, and I totally enjoyed it. I couldn't believe it." She became eager to apply the lesson to her legal work. "I'm a person who always worked as hard as possible, and the idea of relaxing into my work was a real breakthrough for me—not to mention the fact that a by-product of the enjoyment was increased efficiency. I came to understand what it meant to bring full attention and full awareness and full energy to your work.

"I tended to work on two tracks that run at the same time. There's the job at hand, and there's the background chatter. I talk to myself—'Why did he do this? What's going on around here? What do they really want from me?' and so on. The skillful means practice helped me identify the negative patterns and the background noise that had diverted my energy from the work. And so, I began enjoying it more and more. I realized that you have control and can *choose* to enjoy your work more."

Someone who used to react emotionally to provocations of all kinds, Susan says that now she is usually aware enough to get some distance from a situation before responding. "I just step back. And I find that what I end up discussing with the person is totally different from what the content would have been if I'd just reacted."

MINDFULNESS TRIGGERS

Both Susan, the San Francisco litigator, and plaintiff's attorney Warren Anderson of Jacksonville Beach have ways of reminding themselves to wake up and be mindful. Susan has the word "Breathe" taped to her telephone, so that every time it rings she sees it and reestablishes her awareness in the moment. Anderson uses the telephone as a mindfulness trigger, too, but his approach is to let it ring twice, giving him enough time to focus on his breath and get present before answering. Both say it puts them in a much better state of mind for dealing with whatever may come across the wire.

If you look around, you'll find that the world is full of things that can act as triggers for mindfulness. Stop signs and stoplights could hardly be any more obvious in their demand that you make yourself still for a moment. If you choose to heed their demand, they can transform the experience of being caught in traffic from an ordeal into a meditation in motion.

You can program the screen saver on your computer to flash you a reminder, ask your secretary to rap lightly on your office door at random intervals, put your watch on the opposite wrist from what you're used to so that you can't check the time automatically and will be forced to come to attention to find it.

Be creative, and try things until you find what works best for you. How about stopping to breathe and reconnect every time you record your billable time? How about before every meeting, negotiation, or settlement conference?

TRANSFORMING YOUR PRACTICE

Practicing mindfulness can have extraordinary benefits for lawyers. Not only is it a way to live more fully, moment to moment, day to day, but it also can help you do your job better. When you are silent and still, cultivating wakefulness, you free yourself to see more than you otherwise would, often more than the other side sees. And because you are awake in the moment, you have greater latitude in how you're going to handle the next moment.

By helping you recognize and get past the fears, beliefs, and opinions that get in the way of listening well, mindfulness helps you hear more of what your client is really saying, allowing you to bring the broadest possible perspective to a case. This can have an impact on winning.

But more important, in being mindful, you can reclaim your life. You can be there more—and in a deeper way—for your family, for yourself, for your colleagues, and for your clients. It improves concentration and allows you to work with your own mind to foster creativity and innovation. And when you take care of yourself by regularly dropping into non-doing, when you stop striving for even one brief moment, you open the door to your inner life and nourish parts of yourself that want nothing more than to simply *be* in the moment.

Here are some ways of making mindfulness part of your law practice and your life:

• Make a point of noticing how much mental time you spend in the future—in meetings before you get there, in the office when you're playing with your kids, in another city when you haven't left home yet.

A Law Firm with Presence

You don't have to tell Brenda Fingold that mindfulness is a boon for lawyers. "When I'm meditating regularly and focusing on being mindful, I'm more productive and creative in my work," she says. "I also deal much more effectively with daily challenges."

Fingold, the partner in charge of training and professional development at Boston's 360-lawyer Hale and Dorr, was instrumental in making H and D the first law firm in the country to offer a mindfulness-based stress-reduction course for its lawyers. Forty-two associates and partners signed up in the fall of 1998, committing to a two-hour session once a week for eight weeks.

Reactions to the course, Fingold says, were uniformly positive. Not only have participants told her that it reduced their stress levels, but many say it changed their perspective on life. It also contributed to developing more of a sense of community within the firm. "The program gave the participants a chance to relate to each other in a way that doesn't always occur in the course of daily business," she says. "And many have developed stronger relationships as a result. One person told me that whenever she sees one of the others, it reminds her to take a moment to stop and breathe. The participants are walking reminders for each other of their ability to be present."

Jennifer Snyder, a senior partner in the private client area, says the course improved her ability to focus on the task at hand and not get distracted by other pressing matters. "As a result of the course, I am better able to notice each moment and take advantage of what it offers for my work and life."

The course instructor, Ferris Urbanowski of the Center for Mindfulness at the University of Massachusetts Medical School, was hugely impressed with her first-ever group of lawyer-students. "They have a phenomenal ability to concentrate," she says. "And they follow instructions impeccably. They really have a great gift for learning the practice."

Hale and Dorr plans to offer the training again, for staff as well as attorneys.

- Spend five minutes a day cultivating inner stillness.
- Be mindful of the quality of your presence and how it affects other people. Are you keyed up? Distracted? Bursting with energy? Bored?

- Let yourself not know. Try it first on something in which the stakes are not very high. See what it feels like to be in uncertainty. See where it leads.
- When you arrive in the office, really be there as you greet each person. Make eye contact and smile.
- Ask yourself whether your body and your mind are on speaking terms. If not, what might put them back in touch? What would it take for you to actually "inhabit" your body more?
- Try to see your work—for better and for worse—as a way to enrich your inner life.
- When you find yourself being judgmental, try instead to be discerning. Look deeply into whatever captures your attention, and try to see it clearly and precisely, to understand its qualities and its purpose. This is a wonderful lawyerly skill that can be honed to great precision. Unfortunately, it is too often sabotaged by the tendency to judge rather than to really see.
- Keep in mind that efficiency and enjoyment are not mutually exclusive—in fact, they make a potent combination.
- Make a determined effort to be present even for the things you have come to do mechanically. When you answer the phone for the twenty-seventh time today, *really be there with answering the phone for the twenty-seventh time.* When you draft a simple incorporation for the twelfth time this month, *really be there with drafting that simple incorporation.* You may just be surprised by what you find in that moment, now that you're aware.
- Whenever you realize that your mind is off someplace else, don't get down on yourself. Try to be grateful for the awareness, and go on being as present as you can.

CHAPTER SIX

THE TIME-OUT PRACTICE

. . . we hope to find our safety, our belonging
and our healing by increasing our levels of accomplishment.
But our frantic busyness actually makes us deaf
to what is healing and sacred, both in ourselves
and in one another.

—*Wayne Muller*
Legacy of the Heart

EVERY AFTERNOON, SANDRA, a big-city lawyer in the upper Midwest, takes a walk through the park near her office.

At first, she focuses her attention on the sensations in her feet as they touch the ground, lift, and step, letting distractions go when they appear, seeking a certain level of inner quiet. Once she attains it, usually after five or ten minutes, she focuses on the details of the world around her in all their seasonal variety.

Sandra's goal is to tune into the minutiae in her surroundings. She is less interested in the tableau of a lovely day in the park than she is in the odd angle of a single tulip petal as it bends back from the center of the flower. She likes watching people, too, focusing on the way, say, a young man's hand rests on his girlfriend's shoulder, bunching up the wool of her cornflower-blue sweater.

Even in winter Sandra goes out and opens her awareness to the park's rich detail, admiring how the snow hugs the banks of the park's pond and how the wind flattens the tops of the drifts. After a while she begins her walk back to the office, now relaxed, just letting her mind be as open as possible to thoughts and sensations, neither judging nor becoming attached to anything that arises in her mind.

Is she playing hookey? Turning her back on colleagues and clients? Not at all. Sandra is quite clear about what she gets from her walks and what she takes back to the office. The walks slow her down and bring her attention into her body, allowing her to get involved—intimately involved—in the world around her by sensitizing her to nuance. They open and relax her mind so that she can take more in when she returns to work. Taking a time-out in the middle of her day gives Sandra the energy and clarity to carry on, renewed and revived.

She simply refuses to accept that the kind of calm she feels during her rare vacations can't be found at any other time or in any other place. The walks make her happy, her life fuller. And because she designed her routine to meet her own needs, she sees it as a form of self-expression. Finally, her daily walks prevent her from becoming resentful about being cooped up with people who make demands on her. When she returns to the office, she feels ready to resume her work. Having done something for herself, she is once again ready to help other people.

DEVELOPING THE TIME-OUT PRACTICE

Like Sandra, everybody needs a place to retreat to regularly in order to maintain a sense of identity and connection to the larger world. But many lawyers see such breaks as an impossible luxury. Perhaps that's because they don't realize the restrictions they put on themselves. These retreats needn't take a lot of time for you to get a lot from them. Like mindfulness practice, it's much less about how long you do it than *how* you do it; your intent and the quality of your presence make all the difference. And time-outs are amenable to creativity, to personalizing. In fact, the more you tailor your retreat—let's call it your Walden, in honor of Henry David Thoreau, that great connoisseur of solitude—in order to meet your own needs and idiosyncrasies, the more you'll get out of it.

If, in your busy legal career, your Walden becomes as hard to find as Waldo is in those children's books in which the bespectacled young fellow is hiding somewhere on each cluttered page, then it's time to *slow down* and take stock of the situation. Slowness allows us to get some perspective. And, according to novelist Milan Kundera, it beckons memory; the faster we move, the less we remember of what matters to us.

Think about it. You're walking down the street, and something touches off a memory. But it's just off on the periphery of consciousness, hard to discern, alluring but evasive. You want to capture it, bring it back to life in the moment. What do you do? Without even thinking, you slow your pace. It's what we all do, unconsciously. It helps you turn inward so that you can remember.

Maybe, just maybe, it's your Walden calling you back. To the steam room, the ceramic studio, or a nearby café; to the sea, or just to a bench in the park.

Wherever it is, going there is hardly a luxury. It's like the air you breathe (though you may have held your breath for a long, long time). It's a portal. An opening to the terrain of your mothballed dreams, a chance to get the long view of your life, to see it whole and understand where your legal career fits into a much larger picture than you acknowledge day to day.

The Pain of Failing to Reflect

Over the past twenty-five years, the author and speaker Richard Leider made a habit of interviewing people who had retired from successful and distinguished careers with leading companies. Having interviewed more than one thousand of these people, he found that, practically without exception, they say the same things about their lives and what they've learned about living.

First, they say that if they could live their lives over again, they would be more reflective. "They got so caught up in the doing, that they missed the meaning," Leider has written. "They overwhelmingly wished they had stopped at regular intervals to look at the big picture."

This suggests that the natural rhythm of life—the most satisfying rhythm—is one built upon some variant of the action-reflection-action pattern, tailored to fit each individual's unique circumstances. It's safe to say that these days, such rhythms tend to get subverted by the sheer momentum of events and by the often unexamined assumption that doing things is the sole measure of our lives.

When you're a lawyer, doing things—that is, getting things done—consumes most of your time. You set goals and you achieve them; problem solved, hours billed. That's well and good, but it is time to direct more of your attention to accomplishing a new goal: finding a rhythm based on both action and reflection that works for you, so that you don't miss out on much of what is good and nourishing in your practice and in your life.

Without reflection, you run the risk of becoming a person wholly defined by what you do. What you *are* becomes irrelevant. William Byron, S.J., put it this way: "If you are what you do, when you don't you aren't." Think about what it might mean if you were to become ill and couldn't work. Think about what might happen when you retire. What would you have to fall back on? Money? Perhaps *that* would become the core of your identity. If you don't take time for reflection, though, to look at what your life means apart from what you do—you will be in peril of ending up like one of those sad old guys whose lives have become a sorry monologue of stories from the old days, tales of glorious accomplishments, accounts of how they showed so-and-so not to mess with them, and so on and on. Such people don't know who they are, only who they were, and even that was built upon the flimsiest of foundations—ephemeral achievements.

With this terribly sad figure in mind to caution you, it is crucial that you realize that only you can give yourself the permission to find and regularly spend time at your Walden. Only you can learn how to tap into that place not only when you are on vacation, but also during work hours. "We all need to pause before the contemplation of our lives before we can laugh or cry," wrote the poet William Carlos Williams, who then added, "We are dying for it, literally dying for it." The death Williams refers to is not only the literal death of the body from the ill health effects associated with living too fast without taking time to relax, but also the figurative death of that part of you that needs regular reflection to keep it alive. Williams knew, and you should too, that the need to pause is in fact a need, one you disregard at your own substantial risk.

George Kaufman knows something about that need. The veteran of an incredibly varied legal career, he is also director of the Omega Foundation, a center for holistic studies in Rhinebeck, New York. Over the last four years, he's developed a program for lawyers on balancing life and work. "I work on helping them figure out who they are rather than simply letting society tell them who they are," he says. "Mindfulness in all of its forms, relaxation exercises, breathing exercises—anything that brings them into more direct contact with themselves and makes it so that they can no longer hide behind work is helpful. There's no question that there is often a surrendering of the self in the process of practicing law today."

Recalling the Moments

Everyone has had a Walden experience at one time or another—times of feeling connected to what matters most to you, times when you can feel the "shoulds" and the "have tos" of your life melting away and a deeper strength coming through. Think about sitting barefoot on the beach with a good friend, feeling the coolness of the sand and the wind in your hair, listening to and feeling the power of the pounding surf. Wanting only to be here, with someone you trust, bearing witness as your life becomes clearer in its contours and color. If you have had such a moment—alone or with a companion—you can have it again. You can intentionally call it to mind on a workday when you choose to have lunch by yourself, choose to enjoy your food, to eat slowly and deliberately, and to leave work at the office and let feelings and meanings arise as they will, or will not. The important thing is this dipping into the current of your inner life.

You can do it back at the office too, by gazing at a picture you keep close by, a captivating rendition of the scenery you love most—mountains, a seascape, a cactus-studded desert, or a sweeping view of an ancient walled city. Or you can stand before your office window and, settling into the moment, gaze out at the city below, just watching, noticing the people, the flow of cars, the marvelous complexity of the built environment. You can take a walk a few blocks down to the river or the lake just to watch the water move and to be alone with your thoughts.

For Jason, a litigator in a large southern city, taking time out during the day serves a very specific purpose: to free him from the yoke of the billable hour. He has different ways of doing that. Sometimes he watches the river flow. Sometimes he just sits someplace where he isn't likely to see anyone he knows. He finds that it doesn't really matter what he does as long as it's slow enough and quiet enough that he can pay attention to freeing himself from the feeling that he has to make every minute count toward his quota. Jason finds his Walden in these moments.

It is diabolically easy to plug along at your law practice, working long hours, putting out innumerable fires, and fail to notice that it has been months or even years since you looked up to see a spray of stars against the night sky. Time in nature, for many people, is inherently healing. It was certainly so for Thoreau, who spent hours each day "sauntering through the woods and over the fields," getting a sense of himself and his place in the universe that he could never find in the city.

But the benefits of nature are not limited to those who have surplus hours to spend away from the pressures of work and home. Research has shown that sitting before a roaring fire reduces stress, perhaps because it brings us back to the natural world that we evolved to live in. The same is true of gazing at a fish tank, and stroking a pet lowers your blood pressure and stimulates feelings of love and warmth. And there is so much more—the sound of raindrops on a rooftop or the sheer power of the life force pushing a tuft of grass up through the cracks in the sidewalk. All these things can remind you—if you let them—that your world, your work, your family, and your worries all are part of a mysterious and awesome whole. Reflecting on that—being able to glimpse a bit of Walden in the weeds outside your office door and in the awesome strength of a client's love for her son—is to allow yourself to be present to the world you've made and the greater world that you didn't make, and to know yourself as part of both, not just the smaller one.

Lawyers commonly complain that they don't get much opportunity to simply sit and think—even about their work. They used to, in the days before fax machines and E-mail and overnight delivery gave them no place to hide from the perceived urgency of each and every matter. If they can't find the time to think about work-related matters, it isn't likely that they are finding it for personal reflection.

But they should—and so should you—because time given to such reflection is deepening, and you can't help but bring that depth back to work—in the form of compassion for others and the path they are on, and in a broader context in which to view your work.

SETTING A NEW RHYTHM

It is crucial to find Walden moments in your day, brief reminders of who you are. At times, though, it can be maddeningly difficult to cut through the chaos to the gentle spring in the metaphorical wood. One thing that can help is what Stephan Rechtschaffen, M.D., calls "timeshifting," a process that he explains in detail in his book of the same name. No longer a practicing physician, Rechtschaffen recalls times when he witnessed the clash of opposing rhythms in his medical practice. For example, he would enter an examination room to see a patient immediately after dealing with a life-or-death emergency. He wasn't where he needed to be. "The patient needed me to be in a certain rhythm, a comforting and caring rhythm, and I'd come in racing and unable to really be there with her," he says. But he learned to shift into a more appropriate rhythm. "And when I did," he says, "my communication with the patient deepened, and she really felt that I was there for her. It also became much easier, when I was in sync with the patient, to find the root cause of whatever the problem was."

The idea of timeshifting grew out of such experiences. Through them, Rechtschaffen began to understand the power of entraining—the process by which we fall "into sync with another person, object, sound, mood, or rhythm." Using timeshifting to relearn how to relate to time involves a two-step process, beginning with becoming aware of the present moment—that is, *becoming present*—and then becoming aware of the moment's "rhythm and flow."

Timeshifting is a mindfulness practice of sorts because without mindful awareness, you cannot choose to entrain yourself to a new rhythm, one more in keeping with your need for calm and reflection. If you are entrained to the rhythm of city traffic or to the mood of the contentious meeting you just left, pausing for a moment just to check in with yourself may prove to be rather difficult.

But if you can become aware of the rhythm to which you're entrained, you can "downshift" into something more satisfying. To find a rhythm in keeping with inner reflection, you might use music—something soothing and centering—to facilitate a turning inward. A simple, and often ideal, shift may come about by simply entraining to your own breath. At first you may be breathing rather quickly, particularly if you've just finished a difficult meeting or phone conversation, but when you become aware of it, your breath will slow down and bring you back to your natural cadence.

Another useful technique is to create what David Kundtz, author of *Stopping*, calls a "stillpoint." It's a way of creating a rejuvenating respite for yourself, a breather, even if you've got only a minute or less. Here's how it works. First, you stop what you're doing, close your eyes, and take a deep, relaxed breath. Then focus your attention inward, and think of a belief or a conviction that inspires you ("All of life is a chance to learn and grow," might be one), or something for which you feel grateful, or simply summon to mind the face of someone whose presence puts you at peace.

You can do it while in traffic or on the subway, at the water cooler or in the moments before a committee meeting starts, anywhere and any time. The real value, Kundtz says, is cumulative. The more stillpoints you put in your day, the calmer and more peaceful you'll feel.

Moments of stillness help you step outside the flow of time, says Jon Kabat-Zinn. The calmness and relaxation you experience by letting go of time, he explains, helps transform your experience when you go back to it. "Then it becomes possible to flow along with time during your day rather than constantly fighting against it or feeling driven by it, simply by bringing awareness to present-moment experience."

Make a point of taking these moments—moments outside of your work rhythm—at least a couple times a day. Learn to shift intentionally into a reflective rhythm, to become aware of the world beyond the office. Be creative. It's not always easy to do, but it is deeply rewarding. It is a way to grow at work, and not just through the work itself, but in the small breaks between tasks and obligations. These are little Waldens, mini-retreats away from the rhythm of work and into the wilderness inside you. To paraphrase Robert Frost, you may have miles to go (and much to do) before you sleep, but there is freshly fallen snow on the ground outside. Have a good, long look.

Transforming Your Practice

Breaks from the rhythm of work, of whatever length, can be useful times to ponder your own criteria for success. The more time you make for stillness and reflection, the more those criteria are likely to evolve. But whether or not they change—and it's not something you can force—it's a good idea to take them out of the background of assumption and into the light of conscious awareness.

Perhaps you have entrained to the prevailing energy, adopted the prevailing yardsticks, and let money earned or hours billed become your primary criterion for success. Bringing a deeper awareness to your day by making sure to move inward on a regular basis can help you determine whether you have taken on someone else's—perhaps the dominant culture's—criteria and let you begin to reassess your standards for success.

If you find that you have lost contact with your personal touchstones, then even small breaks in your day can help you reconnect. The mere act of punctuating your hours with mini-reprieves is a way of staking out your own ground and reestablishing a sense of your own integrity.

As you reassess your standards for success, you might consciously look for an alternative to the language of dollars and cents—and winning and losing—perhaps in the concepts of wholeness and caring, community and love. At the very least, those ideas offer a context in which to gauge the contribution you make as you move through your professional life.

Here are some additional ways to make the time-out practice a part of your life:

- Be clear with yourself about what or where your Walden is. Assuming you have one, do you retreat to it often enough?
- Next time you find yourself waiting—for the dentist or for a train—instead of thinking of the time as wasted, try to see it as "found" time.
- Keep an impressionistic journal—writing only two or three vivid sentences a day—to record your explorations of the wilderness inside you.
- Try to notice how the rhythm of the moment changes as you go through your day. Experiment with consciously altering it.

tional evasion; it's just that he needs some help. What might happen if you paused for a moment and recounted David Link's story about the client who wanted to sell his trucking company, and Charlie who wasn't so sure? Can you see how it might lead to a turning point in the case? The client may assure you that you've already hit rock-bottom truth; on the other hand, it may be exactly the permission he needs to tell you what is really going on, who it is you're actually representing.

From Adversary to Healer

It used to be that one of the great things about being a lawyer was the number of roles you could play in your clients' lives. You could be a counselor, a trusted adviser, a problem solver, or even a peacemaker. In theory, you still can. The reality, however, is somewhat different: the lawyer as zealous advocate has eclipsed all the other possible roles, and what was once thought of as *legal* ethics is now almost entirely adversarial ethics. Clearly, there are times when advocating on behalf of a client in an adversarial forum is a great and noble role for a lawyer to play, but it is crucial that it not become the only role.

While alternative dispute resolution has made encouraging inroads over the last twenty years, the adversarial system continues to hover above ADR like an elephant over a chipmunk. Fortunately, a growing number of lawyers are chafing under the adversarial harness, feeling that it offers an impoverished view both of the legal system and of human nature. Being ill at ease with making it the default approach to solving disputes, they are looking for ways to bring other dimensions of reality—and other methodologies—into the process. Their goal is to work for a greater good, not for the narrow and often Pyrrhic victories that an unfettered adversarial impulse so frequently brings about.

It has often been said that the law is one of the great healing professions, that while medicine heals the body and the clergy heals the soul, the law heals societal rifts. David Link believes it is time for lawyers to reclaim their role as healers, which extensive historical research tells him was in fact the original role of lawyers—or the people who eventually came to be known as lawyers. As far as we can tell, Link says, lawyers' precursors first appeared after hunter-gatherers began settling in villages and disputes started to arise over who had the right to use a particular piece of property. The wisest man or woman around would adjudicate, and as civilization progressed, the decisions were written down. That became village law. Eventually, people began acting as representatives of disputing parties. But they were not adversaries; they were trying to bring peace back to the village. The "lawyer's" responsibility was not only to his "client" but also to the entire community.

Rob Lehman is president of the Fetzer Institute in western Michigan, a philanthropic organization dedicated to exploring connections between mind, body, and spirit. A lawyer himself, he recalls a time when a deep inner connection characterized communities' relationships to their lawyers. "I grew up in a town of three thousand where we had two doctors and two lawyers," he says. "And I always thought of the lawyer as somewhat similar to the doctor. You went to the lawyer for a problem, and that lawyer would really help. You really looked to the lawyer in town as someone of enormous stature and respect, and that person in some way could help you through life's problems and crises in more than just a technical way. And I think there was almost an implicit, almost inchoate healing character of the lawyer in our tradition, certainly in the idea of the wise counselor and listening person."

In fact, it may not be too far-fetched to hypothesize a kind of collective cultural memory of a time when lawyers were healers. It's a notion that might explain some of the pain of living—as Lehman describes contemporary lawyers' dilemma—"above the surface and alone," when the resources needed to achieve a more satisfying professional life remain primarily *below* the surface. If the profession has strayed far from its ancient roots, perhaps it's because healing requires certain *inner* tools, most of which are neglected today. "If wisdom is about healing, I think it's all right there encoded in what we've done," says Lehman. "We just need to unpack it in some way and rediscover it."

To help lawyers unpack their history, the Fetzer Institute has created the Healing and the Law Project, a program designed to explore just what it means to be a lawyer-healer and to foster deeper understanding and promotion of that role. Interestingly, the program itself is the fruit of a healing experience. It grew out of a legal dispute between the Institute and a law firm it had engaged to handle a particular transaction. Just as things were heating up and the parties neared being drawn into the vortex of litigation, an Institute trustee reminded both sides that healing is fundamental to what the Institute stands for. He proposed a settlement whereby the law firm would donate a sum of money to a Fetzer-funded program on how the law can contribute to healing, which they agreed to do.

The program calls for a nationwide search for stories that demonstrate lawyers' capacity for healing (an effort directed by Link) as well as conferences, books, and perhaps a culminating PBS program akin to Bill Moyers's *Healing and the Mind*, in which Fetzer also played an instrumental role.

To Cure or to Heal?

Another story Link tells does a great job of showing what it looks like when a lawyer sees himself as a healer. The story also serves as Link's answer to a question he is often asked: "But what if your client wants you to be an attack dog, not a healer?" The incident, which Link says he has verified, occurred a few years ago and concerns a Notre Dame alumnus who was once Link's student (a fact that gives him no small amount of pleasure). Link tells it like this:

> This lawyer had a client come to him and say that he'd had a breakdown in a business relationship with another guy, and he thought the guy broke an agreement they'd had.
>
> "I want you to sue the guy," he told him. "I want you to take him for everything he's worth." He was mad, and he really wanted to get him.
>
> So, the lawyer said, "Well, have you talked settlement on this? Generally I like to talk settlement before I . . ."
>
> "No," he said, "I don't want you to have settlement talks or anything else. I want you to sue him." Then he said he had a great idea. "Christmas is coming," he told the lawyer. "I want you to serve court papers on him on Christmas Eve."
>
> The lawyer was aghast. "Christmas Eve?" he said. "You're going to make him *miserable*."
>
> "Yeah," the client told him, "I want to get that sonofabitch. I just want to grind it into him."
>
> The lawyer paused for a moment, then he said, "Not only are you going to make him miserable, but you're going to make his family, his wife and kids, miserable too."
>
> "Yep," he responded. "That's right. Let's do it."
>
> But the lawyer had more to say. He said, "You know, you're also going to make yourself miserable."
>
> "No, I won't," the client responded. "Nothing's going to make me happier."

"Then, you're going to have to go down the street," the lawyer told him. "You'll have to get another lawyer, because I won't do that. In fact, I don't file lawsuits unless we've at least had some conversation about settlement. And I'm sure not going to file anything on anyone on Christmas Eve."

"There's no time running on this," he continued, "and if I take your case, you get to make all the decisions. But I'm not going to take your case. It's just not the kind of work I do."

"But you've always represented me," the client answered. "You're my regular lawyer, and I want you to do this."

"If you want to do it this way," the lawyer told him, "I'm not going to do it."

It was quiet for a minute or so, and then the lawyer said, "I'll tell you what I'll do: if you wait until after Christmas—and I mean well after Christmas, after the kids have gone back to school—then I will file whatever lawsuit you want, but I'm going to insist that when we file that lawsuit, we do it as a means to spur settlement discussions. The court's going to require that anyway, and I'm going to require it. And those are the conditions under which I'll do this. And I'm not doing anything before Christmas."

With that, the client stormed out of the office, furious at his lawyer. After Christmas, he returned to the office.

"Do you want me to file those papers?" the lawyer asked.

He said, "No, I've been thinking about what you said, and you're right. I would have been miserable if I'd done that. And you're right, he's not such a bad guy after all. And I'd kind of like to patch things up. In fact, I wouldn't mind continuing in this relationship and maybe kind of square what happened here, and I'd like to try to keep the relationship together and make some kind of settlement on this one mistake. Why don't you talk to his lawyer and see if we can patch this thing back up."

As Link points out, this story gets at an important distinction that is often missed, that between curing and healing. "In medicine, it's possible to treat something, to actually even cure it, but never heal it. On the other hand, you can heal incurable diseases. You can heal the people, even if the disease isn't cured. You might heal them; you might bring them to peace. It's the same thing in law: there's a big difference between getting to a solution to the problem and healing the people involved. That's what these two guys were involved with, these two businesspeople. They had a social conflict. There was an illness there.

You could have brought about a cure by separating them. The problem goes away, but you may not have healed either one of them."

Link contrasts the lawyer as healer—an orientation he believes a great many lawyers would find deeply satisfying—with an adversarial mind-set that says, "I'm just a hired gun. You tell me you want to hurt the other guy in court, I'll hurt him in court." The problem, he says, is that now the easiest thing to sell is, "I'll be your representative, and I'll do anything you want." It's a version of "The client is always right." But it is also, he points out, a version of the client-as-customer. "I think we should be seeing the client as more like a patient," Link explains.

"Somebody recently said to me, 'You know, we've gone from being the people who used to break up the street fights to being the people who are now the surrogate street fighters. We used to be the people who tried to bring about peace for our client. And now we're the bright people who extend the war.'"

Extending the war is not the answer. Building connections is. Moving toward healing in your law practice requires developing an integrative approach to lawyering, understanding the kinds of concepts that only recently were seen as soft and touchy-feely in the field of medicine but no longer are. Research from many sources—medicine, public health, physics—shows that whatever connects is healing; what separates can be lethal. Even quantum physics tells us that nothing in the universe exists as an independent "thing"; all of us are connected by what physicist Werner Heisenberg calls "a complicated tissue of events, in which connections of different kinds alternate or overlap or combine and thereby determine the texture of the whole."

To view law as a healing profession means to bring it into line with what is becoming increasingly clear in other disciplines: that fomenting war, which almost invariably *dis*integrates, runs counter to the natural inclinations of humankind and to the movements of the physical universe.

TRANSFORMING YOUR PRACTICE

Opportunities to expand awareness and to heal are everywhere in the law: in a client's subtle hints that she really wants a reason to do the right thing, the less hurtful thing, in a dispute; in the behavior of the lawyer on the other side, whose apoplectic rage hides a need to escape from a process that has become a prison; in the elegance and simplicity of a solution locked inside the head of a young associate, who is too frightened to share it with her supervising partner; and in the emotional turmoil of a client who has come in for a will and who obviously needs to talk about his painful estrangement from his children.

Allowing clients and colleagues to tell their stories is to allow them to begin the work of integration, to start to put themselves back together and heal relationships that may have come apart. Alan Minuskin, a faculty member in the civil litigation clinic at Boston College Law School, knows the value of simply bearing witness in this way. "Often, when you're representing people below the poverty line, they come in terrified and distrustful, and dignity can take a long time to cultivate," he says. "But sometimes you have this moment of transcendence, of arrival, when the client suddenly feels that he's been dignified by being able to share this heavy burden with someone. It can be kind of like a religious moment, and there's only you and this other person sharing it."

Once you have established healing as your goal, you can move clients in that direction in a number of ways. One very simple thing to keep in mind, though, is a lesson that the medical profession has only recently begun to learn, now that research can be called upon to verify it: the mere presence of a physician tends to have a healing influence on sick patients. What if you were to take this into consideration in the moments before you meet with each client? What if, realizing that your very presence can have either a salutary or a corrosive effect, you were to begin the interaction ready to use your best approximation of a good bedside manner?

You can further enhance the potential for healing in any number of ways, including the following:

- Make it clear that healing can in fact become the goal of your collaboration.
- Enlist the client's help in determining what would constitute a healing result.
- Refuse to take the adversarial role as your center.
- Advocate for the deepest, truest interest of the client that you are aware of, rather than just for the surface emotions they present, such as anger or vengefulness. (You can even help clients heal on the physical level by pointing out that chronic anger and hostility

has been shown in study after study to increase chances of heart attack and premature death.)

- Realize that your client is probably in transition—ending something and moving into a time of new beginnings. Ask "What steps can we take to set you on a positive path of growth?"
- Seek to understand the client in his or her familial, occupational, and social contexts. It's hard to really understand anyone's needs if you don't understand the ways in which they are connected to the wider world.
- Seek to understand the client's spiritual life (if he or she cares to share this information). It may offer clues to what kind of approaches and outcomes would be most healing. For example, might forgiveness play a significant part in resolving the dispute?
- Open yourself to the possibility that what the client needs may be either wider than or simply different from what you presume. Then allow the client to express what he or she really wants.
- Understand the healing power that comes when you advocate for the client as a whole and unique human being, rather than merely as an interesting legal problem or just another file to close.
- Understand the healing power of listening (see Chapter 8).
- Realize that clients really do want more than just a legal fix and that they come to you because they want to feel more whole and at peace.
- Encourage the client to get the emotional support he or she needs.
- Help the client find the real human meaning behind the legal problem.

The list could go on. And on. What is important to remember is that being a healer is an attitude, not a specific technique. If and when you decide that it's the path that feels right for you, the way to get there will become clearer as you go along. Certainly all the practices described up till now, as well as those that follow, make a great deal of sense in the context of preparing to act as a healer. Anything that helps you cultivate awareness, compassion, inner strength, balance, and self-knowledge will be an ally on the path of healing and the law. So will an ear for stories, particularly the kind that make hidden meanings suddenly plain and the world itself seem a warmer, more inviting place.

For more information on the Fetzer Institute's Healing and the Law Project, contact:

Fetzer Institute
9292 West KL Avenue
Kalamazoo, MI 49009
(616) 375-2000
E-mail: info@fetzer.org

CHAPTER EIGHT

THE LISTENING PRACTICE

All things in the world want to be heard,
as do the many voices inside us.
—Frederic and Mary Ann Brussat
Spiritual Literacy

JAMES NELSON, FORMERLY CHIEF judge of the Los Angeles Municipal Court, is a lucky man: he learned the power of listening on his first day on the bench, in small-claims court, where they sent all the new people. "I had a case in which a lady had sued a dry cleaner for damaging her clothing," he recalls. "Well, when she got through presenting her case, I wasn't even clear about whether or not she was suing the right dry cleaner. She just didn't seem to have a case. So as soon as she was done, I said that the judgment was for the defendant.

"At that point, the dry cleaner almost attacked me. I thought he was going to jump over the bench and grab me, so I said, 'Sir, sir, I just ruled in your favor. The case is over.' But he was furious. He said, 'I wanted to tell you about what this woman did!' And at that moment, I realized that most people would rather be heard than win."

Today Nelson believes there is a spiritual principle involved in hearing people. It might be stated like this: Although adjudication may represent the *cure* to a legal problem, the *healing* often remains incomplete until the parties feel they have actually been heard. When they need to be *heard*, merely "hearing" their case is not enough. To put it back in the law office context, if clients need to be heard, merely listening to their "problems," as presented, will rarely do the trick.

It may seem odd at first to call something as ordinary as listening a spiritual practice. But that's probably because listening really well is anything but ordinary. How many people have you known who had that skill? How did you feel when you were with them? In fact, spirituality without listening is hard to imagine. If you're looking for answers, for meaning, for a direction in life, you can't possibly find what you're after without listening, both to the myriad "voices" in the world around you and to the inner language of your instincts and yearnings. As with other spiritual practices, you can cultivate the ability to listen well, but, in the end, it is only partly about doing. It's more a function of who you are, how willing you are to be present with others, and how sensitive you are to what can be accomplished when you really listen.

Survey after survey has shown that what clients look for in lawyers goes well beyond technical proficiency and includes a real sense that the lawyer cares about their problems. Not only that, but a huge percentage of lawyer disciplinary actions can be traced to a failure to listen. Isn't that really what it's about when clients complain that their lawyers fail to return their phone calls?

What's gone wrong? Well, research shows a thing or two that may help get to the root of the problem. In an article entitled "On Being Human" in *Law Practice Management* magazine, law firm management consultant Merrilyn Astin Tarlton distills down to two points what a variety of studies have made inescapably clear: (1) clients crave supportive, productive human relationships with good lawyers; and (2) lawyers feel isolated from supportive, productive human relationships. Clearly, lawyers and clients have a lot in common. Perhaps they should get to know each other better. Tarlton goes on:

> We each bring a unique perspective and experience to any interaction. You have your years of legal education and experience. Your client has an understanding of his or her situation, personal style and expecta-

resolve the problem that is outside your experience. Let yourself be open to signs of wisdom that may bear fruit.

- LISTENING TO HELP THE CLIENT HEAR HIMSELF: This is where the practice known as active listening can be particularly helpful. By feeding back to the client what it is you think you heard him saying—that is, the *meaning* you think you heard—you give him the opportunity both to clarify what he really meant and, if he is willing, to hear things he may have been unaware of.
- LISTENING FOR THE CLIENT'S OWN LISTENING PROBLEMS: Clients who don't listen can be maddening. They waste time and fail to give useful feedback. Being aware of this problem gives you an opportunity to deal with it—preferably directly, but with tact—before it leads to abject frustration or even rage. And, keep in mind that encouraging clients to become better listeners can pay off. Their experience causes them to pick up on different things from the ones you perceive, things you might miss that could have a direct bearing on the case.
- LISTENING TO YOUR OWN INTUITION: The legal culture doesn't exactly embrace this source of knowledge, but that doesn't mean that your hunches and inklings shouldn't be respected and explored. If your gut tells you something is wrong with the picture, check it out.

When people come to you in crisis, it is almost axiomatic that they need to be healed in some way. Some of that healing—in the form of knowing that someone is truly committed to hearing not only about the facts of the case but also *their feelings about whatever it is that brought them to the office*—is best done before going forward with a legal solution. Then calmer heads can prevail, and the likelihood of finding the right solution for a particular client will increase dramatically.

Listening to Save a Marriage

Ron Supancic has practiced family law in Woodland Hills, California, for more than twenty years. He refuses to take problems at face value, without first probing, listening, and reflecting. He tells the story of a client who, having been traumatized by his first divorce, was watching his second marriage crumble. He and his wife had been to three psychotherapists, all of whom said the marriage was hopeless. When

tions, and preferred method for receiving information. Value this knowledge. Welcome the client into the process of problem solving. View your relationship as a joint effort.

You can do this only if you are willing to listen. That can be difficult in a profession that is all about words—wielding them, packaging them, analyzing them. Too often they are used as walls or weapons, a means of separating the lawyer from others and keeping the relationship merely clinical. If you seek to dazzle clients with your cleverness and brilliance, you end up alienating them and, in the process, losing the opportunity to experience the satisfaction that comes from connecting on a meaningful level.

To begin improving the situation, it may help to return for a moment to the medical analogy. In order to develop the lawyerly equivalent of a good bedside manner, you have to become a good listener. There is no way around it. Active, caring, committed listening is a gift you can give your clients—and giving gifts, rather than perfunctory interest, can get a relationship off to a good start or help mend one that may have lost its way.

A Chicago employment lawyer describes something of an epiphany she had about listening—before, she says, it was too late. "I had a near miss, a potential disaster that showed me I just wasn't listening. I was too busy second-guessing—my family's needs, my colleagues' needs. I was too busy to really hear what they actually needed, and certainly too busy to hear what I needed."

Listening, and feeling heard, are more important than most people seem to realize. For both the speaker and the listener, there are practical, emotional, spiritual, and even physical benefits. Studies conducted by Maryland psychologist and author James J. Lynch, Ph.D., have shown that when we listen to people, it actually lowers their blood pressure. Lynch studied this phenomenon in crying babies, whose blood pressure continued to rise the longer they cried. "Then I realized that's exactly what the adult patients are doing, but their cries are inward," Lynch said in an interview. "And I began to understand that listening to people lowers their blood pressure because we hear their cries."

HEARING THROUGH THE DIN

Sometimes it feels as if no one is listening particularly well these days. Soaring decibels, overscheduled days, worsening traffic, and constant demands that have to be met *right this instant* are just some of the things that make people shut off their receivers and pull inward.

As a lawyer, your problem is probably compounded by the fact that—unless you're a rare case—you were never taught to listen. You were taught to advocate, but your teachers almost certainly neglected to mention that the roots of successful advocacy are in listening. This makes it difficult to advocate for the *whole* client, rather than just for a narrow interpretation of what his or her interests are—that is, for the person rather than simply for the anger or the hurt, or even for the money that may be at stake.

When a Houston lawyer knew his only chance of winning a jury trial in a huge civil liability case was to get jurors to see the humanity in his Fortune 1OO-CEO client—a humanity he had "heard" through a gruff, thick-skinned exterior—he followed his intuition and found the way to the man's heart in his relationship to his deceased father. When the CEO took the stand, his lawyer was able to show the courtroom the "boy who'd lost his daddy," a man who had made him swear on the day he left for college that he would always try to do the right thing.

This could never have happened had the lawyer not listened well enough to hear the young man inside the old man. And it also couldn't have happened if the lawyer wasn't representing his client as a whole person. Seeing something larger at stake than a possible moment of embarrassment, he introduced the father-son relationship at trial in spite of his client's desire that he stay away from it. He ignored the request simply because he believed in his client, and he believed that the promise he had once made to his father really was the key to understanding the man and the way he had handled the event at the center of the case. Many—perhaps most—lawyers would have done as told, particularly if the client was the head of one of the world's largest corporations. This lawyer did not, because in his mind he wasn't representing just a symbol of power; he was representing a human being, one who had been someone's son and who, he believed, had truly tried to do the right thing for everyone involved in a terribly unpleasant situation.

THE CHARACTERISTICS OF LISTENING

Most lawyers see their job as getting to a solution, *fast*. Once they think they've got it, they tend to stop listening. Once the raw facts have gelled into something recognizable, it's time to forge ahead, to do whatever

research is necessary, draft the relevant documents, move satisfying is that, either for you or for the client? It's effic it's also mechanical: fact provider meets with fact analy provides, analyzer analyzes, and presto! a solution is prod the kind of work that makes for happy lawyers or clients.

Really listening means much more than merely acce list of facts at face value and finding in them a pattern th standard solution. It also means:

- LISTENING WITH WHAT ZEN BUDDHISTS C "BEGINNER'S MIND": that is, as if you are listening very first time; everything is new, and nothing is taken
- LISTENING THROUGH THE CLIENT'S ROLE Clients behave according to their own concepts of how *supposed* to behave. That concept acts as a filter, allowin facts, ideas, and feelings to be expressed and others—th to be inappropriate or irrelevant—to be withheld.
- LISTENING IN ORDER TO LEARN FROM THE If you stop as soon as you get "the" answer, you may be yourself off to better options. Perhaps the client knows

Active Listening Exercise

Active listening is a practice whereby you not only maintain while another is speaking, but you also attempt to draw out the with proactive questioning techniques and reflection. It is a that requires, above all, an open mind and heart—and patience the process:

Step 1: Listen to the speaker's description of the matter on his

Step 2: Restate his premise as you understand it, and ask for mation of this understanding.

Step 3: Ask open-ended follow-up questions to deepen your standing. With each response, reflect back your under ing to make sure you're on the same page.

Step 4: If the speaker expresses any emotions, whether dire indirectly, make sure to acknowledge those feelings.

Step 5: Ask the speaker if there is anything else he'd like to sa thank him for sharing his thoughts with you.

the client came to Supancic, his biggest fear was of losing custody of his four-year-old daughter.

Supancic put him in parenting classes, a rage-management program, and divorce counseling (not to be confused with couples counseling). After six months of classes, therapy, and working with Supancic, the client's wife fell in love with him again. "She told me he was transformed," Supancic says. "They got back together and the divorce was set aside—after three therapists said it couldn't be done."

Where someone else might have seen only a "client," Supancic *heard* a man with singular problems and unique potential. Where another person would have seen a brutal custody battle ahead, Supancic *heard* someone capable of taking responsibility for his part in a dying relationship, someone with the ability to act to make things better. And where someone else might have seen little more than the chance to earn a fee, Supancic *heard* an opportunity for personal satisfaction that goes way beyond anything money can buy.

Lawyers like Supancic know the pleasure that comes from crafting creative solutions, the kind designed to work for a *particular* client at a particular moment in his or her life. In fact, some lawyers have described doing such work as an almost ecstatic experience—ecstatic because it brings to bear *all* of your ways of knowing, not only the technical, but also the conceptual, the empathic, and the spiritual. It is work that calls on multiple levels of intelligence, and on occasion—particularly when the gap between being a lawyer and being a human being actually disappears—it is transformative. But it cannot happen—as Supancic well knows—unless you are able to hear the client well enough that his *personhood* rather than just his clienthood becomes clear.

Judging Others

Lawyers tend to judge themselves harshly. After all, they work in a culture that rewards and values winning above everything else, and no one wins every time. Apart from the fact that there is no percentage in being so hard on yourself, self-judging also inhibits good listening. For one thing, it can be hard to hear someone else over the negative chatter in your own head. For another, people who are hard on themselves are often hard on others. And if your goal is to really hear what a client says—or, even better, who he or she *is*—then it is crucial to understand that judgment is deadly.

It's essential that you try to be aware of any tendency to judge the client or yourself. When judgments arise, simply watch and try not to identify with them. Know that you are not your judgments, that if you refuse to get caught up in them, they will dissipate and leave you to the work at hand: being present and open for your client. But awareness is crucial, because if you are unconscious of your tendency to judge, clients may still feel it, and lawyer jokes are but one form of revenge taken against professionals seen as arrogant and imbued with a disturbing sense of their own superiority. Instead, keep in mind that the person sitting across from you is unlike any other on earth. It helps to realize that you, too, are singular. Only by listening well and with devotion can you determine exactly how your unique collaboration can be most beneficial for this particular client in this particular case

Kenneth Cloke, a lawyer-turned-mediator in Santa Monica, California, says the way to appreciate this uniqueness is by listening not just with the head but with the heart, "and not just in your role, but as a human being; and not just by being involved, but by being committed."

 Exercise: Becoming Aware of Judgment

To become a really good listener, it is imperative that you become aware of judgments as they arise. Practice, by entering into conversations intending to notice them. When you do, simply notice. Don't *do* anything.

Once you become aware of your mind's tendency to judge, try to notice how judging affects your ability to listen, what you hear and what you tune out, and how well you're able to empathize.

Then try this technique, from *Dialogue: Rediscover the Transforming Power of Conversation* by Linda Ellinor and Glenna Gerard:

Next time a judgment interferes with your ability to listen, imagine that you are grabbing it in your hand, literally. Then hold it out in front of you, creating a space between yourself and the judgment. You can then continue to listen through that space, allowing the other person's words and reasoning to enter. When another judgment nudges its way into your awareness—as it no doubt will—repeat the process. If you can really make yourself see the space between yourself and the judgment, you can learn to listen with curiosity even to those with whom you disagree.

To explain the difference between being involved and being committed, Cloke offers a joke: What's the difference between ham and eggs? The chicken is involved, but the pig is committed. "I'm talking about listening as if your life depended on it, without any past or any future," he says. "Just listening."

Avoiding Prejudiced Opinions

Santa Fe lawyer Merit Bennett has spent a lot of time thinking about what gets in the way of lawyers' and clients' seeing each other as they really are. On the client's side, he says, there are the expectations that come from a host of cultural clichés: the lawyer as a hired gun without a conscience, as a person who will employ any aggressive tactic to win, and as one who will dispense with honesty on a client's behalf as long as he gets paid.

On the lawyer's side, presuppositions can include the notion that a given client's wishes will not differ significantly from those of other clients who had similar problems. "The natural tendency of my mind to sort through my past experiences and arrive at a common experiential denominator has often caused me to treat the unique human being sitting before me as just another replica of the common denominator and to ignore anything to the contrary," Bennett writes in *Law and the Heart: A Practical Guide for Successful Lawyer/Client Relationships*.

As Bennett notes, it is imperative that lawyers become conscious of their own minds' natural tendency to "reexperience only what we have previously experienced," lest they fail to see who is really sitting in their office and end up living in a kind of perpetual taped replay of the past. Listening becomes impossible under such conditions.

In his own practice, Bennett encourages clients to talk themselves out. He asks questions to help them express themselves and also allows them to explore how they feel about what they are saying. That, he says, is where the gold is.

"They come in with facts and ideas and behavior and all the rest, and after it's all on the table, it's easy for me to play the lawyer and figure out what the legal issue is, analyze it, come up with a course of action, and so on. But what happens behind that—and usually it's in a place the client has not gone—is how they feel about it, about the conduct of the other party, about what has happened to them, and about what kind of an outcome would give them a good feeling."

Once you go there, Bennett says, it's as if you've opened up the door, and the answer just comes. "It comes right out of the client's mouth. Suddenly you see what the real issue is. It's usually not what they came in with. Usually it's about hurt, and I get them to talk about why they are hurt, how to get at it, and how to heal it. Suddenly it resolves itself at a whole other level."

Bennett gives the example of a woman who called him to discuss taking legal action against a priest who had molested her many years earlier. Realizing the statute had run, but also aware that the woman was still carrying tremendous pain resulting from the incident, he decided to talk to her about how she felt about the incident and how it was currently affecting her life. "It came out that she felt this man still had power over her twenty years after the incident," Bennett says. "We were then able to go into what had to happen inside of her so that she could disconnect from his having this power. Of course, I didn't end up taking the case, but we talked for about forty-five minutes, and she answered her own questions. The question had changed from a legal one to one of how to empower her. For me, the lesson of that is that if you keep on talking long enough and really listen, all of a sudden the key will hand itself to you. But you have to hang back a while and not jump into the lawyer mind-set right away."

Bennett takes only a small percentage of the cases that come into his office, but he spends time with each prospective client, without pushing them to reach a result. "If you do push too quickly into a case, and you fail to get to the feelings and the underlying issues, the case will often fall apart down the line. It may happen when the other side makes a motion for summary judgment, and it's because you didn't go far enough—you didn't listen well enough at the outset."

Southern California attorney Carroll Straus points out one of many cases—this one a divorce—in which she realized that really listening can help blow away assumptions that may be detrimental to a client's welfare. "It happened just after I passed the bar, when I took over a case from my predecessor at the firm I joined," she recalls. "The poor client was a Vietnam veteran with post-traumatic stress disorder who had not worked during the marriage. My predecessor had him fighting for spousal support, but I soon figured out that he wanted no such thing. I told my opposing counsel the truth (things were somewhat more collegial and courteous then), and we settled the case. My client's mental state improved markedly, too."

Centering Meditation for Preparing to See a Client

Step 1: Sit comfortably, and become aware of your body, where it is touching the chair, where you feel tension or pain. You needn't do anything; simply notice. Gently close your eyes and watch your breath.

Step 2: Consider the mystery of what is about to occur—the fact that each of you—you and your client—is a unique being and that your interaction, to the extent that it's genuine, will be unprecedented. It will have its own dynamic and contain its own seeds of meaning.

Step 3: Become aware that the moment is brimming with possibilities, that by listening deeply, you may be able to heal; by forgoing judgment, you may be able to see more deeply; by letting yourself be touched, you may be able to convey to the other that he is not alone.

Step 4: Let your mind become quiet. Again, become aware of your breath. Feel your feet on the floor, your body against the chair. Breathe. Slowly open your eyes.

It may be that Straus's lack of experience allowed her to see—and certainly to hear—things that years of practice might have blinded her to. But today she considers herself a holistic lawyer, and she works hard to remain aware of the unique possibilities in every professional encounter.

HARD WORK THAT SATISFIES

Listening well takes work. It requires a willingness to invest time and energy without any guarantee of results. But you get a lot back. "Inevitably," says Bennett, "if you don't take the case, the person will tell other people about you, and you'll get another case. They will tell ten or twenty people that I'm the greatest lawyer around and that I helped them, when all I did was have a conversation and listen."

Becoming a good—ideally, a masterful—listener leads to better relationships with your clients; often better, more satisfying results in your cases; and more enjoyment in your work.

Cloke, the Santa Monica mediator, says you also help to unblock energy, which is invigorating. "When you're listening, it's like a circuit:

energy flows both ways. When you withhold, you block the energy, but when you give through listening, you allow the energy to flow. It takes a lot of intensity and energy to do it, but when you do, you're never bored; you're always fascinated."

Psychologist James Lynch's research on the physiological effects of listening seems to support Cloke's claim. Not only does the research demonstrate that the speaker benefits when listening is occurring, but it also shows that the *listener's* blood pressure drops. So even though listening well is hard work, it is also relaxing. Maybe that's the body's way of saying that it is good to help others—that the need to do so is a basic part of who we are.

TRANSFORMING YOUR PRACTICE

Sometimes just listening to a client is the best thing you can do for her. Indeed, part of being a good listener is knowing when it's appropriate to do no more than that. At such moments, all the client may need is a witness, someone to simply be there—to preside, as it were—as she makes the connections that give rise to a sense of meaning in the situation that brought her to you. Like breathing, listening is something we all do, but in doing it consciously, we can make a tremendous difference in our lives and the lives of others.

And it is crucial that we listen to ourselves all the while. One way of doing that is by paying attention to the stories you tell your children, your nieces and nephews. "Most parents know the importance of telling children their own story, over and over again," writes Rachel Naomi Remen, "so that they come to know in the tellings who they are and to whom they belong."

In thinking about the stories you tell your children, you have a wonderful way of gauging the truth. Consider the stories you tell about yourself, then ask yourself: Are they really about *me*? Do they offer the kinds of meanings that will satisfy a child's hunger to understand who she is and where she comes from? Or am I letting my professional self interfere, by emphasizing my prowess and worldly successes? Do my words convey my *personal* view of my life or an idealized view?

The desire to be true to your children—or your nieces and nephews—can help you determine if, or where, you've lost your path, and not only by examining the stories you tell about yourself. In truth, much of the inner conflict so many lawyers feel may ultimately come down to another child-related question: Is what I do in my daily work consistent with what I teach my children and with the kind of lives I want for them?

Here are a few ways to implement a deeper emphasis on listening in your law practice:

- Consider that listening, in and of itself, is a service you provide your clients, one that speaks to their inner needs.
- Create something new with each client.
- In every case, strive to achieve a resolution that speaks to the client's underlying sense of meaning.
- Allow the rest of the world to melt away so that all you see and hear and want to understand is the client—or potential client—in your office.
- Realize that clients come to you to be heard and that you fail them when you do not hear them.

CHAPTER NINE

THE SERVICE PRACTICE

A great deal of the exhaustion that comes from work can
be attributed to losing sight of the very world we are serving.
—*David Whyte*
The Heart Aroused

I slept and dreamt that life was joy.
I awoke and saw that life was service,
I acted and behold, service was joy.
—*Rabindranath Tagore*

For Richard Halpert, it took a long time to realize that when it came to finding satisfaction in the law, he'd been asking the wrong questions.

Halpert grew up in Michigan, the son of a Polish immigrant father and an American mother who encouraged him to become successful, powerful, and rich. To them, law school seemed to be just the way to get there. A terrific student, he made law review at Indiana University Law School and, after graduating, went to work for one of Chicago's most prestigious law firms.

He hated it. Finding the environment to be sterile, sexist, and avaricious, he returned to Kalamazoo without a job, certain he'd rather load crates at the local winery than work for that kind of firm. He then took a job as a prosecutor, which he enjoyed, but—having a family to support—couldn't make a living at.

So he tried private criminal practice, a period from which his most vivid memories are of getting both a child molester and a contract killer acquitted. "I realized then that if I had any talent, it wasn't for that," he says. "I had come to have some power and prestige, but I wasn't happy. I felt a kind of spiritual deprivation."

Finally, things changed. He took on the case of a troubled young man who had been the driver of a car that was in an accident, killing several passengers, including his sister. By the time Halpert met him, he had become a recluse, tortured by guilt and remorse because he was unable to remember who caused the crash. When Halpert located evidence that proved the young man could not have been at fault, the effect was instantaneous. "He just blossomed," Halpert says.

So did Halpert. He had found his home. Having spent years feeling disconnected from a sense of authenticity in his work, he had tapped into a source of passion and energy that made everything seem possible. "I found that this is where I belonged, helping injured people put their lives together again. I got satisfaction from that like never before."

The question he had been asking, the one that was off the mark and had grown out of his parents' emphasis on money and power, was this: What can the law do for me? Suddenly he realized that the question that enlivened and inspired him was quite a different one: How can I use the law to serve my clients, to help them regain their self-esteem and happiness? "I've learned that the less time I spend focusing on me and the more time I spend focusing on my clients, the happier I become. It's ironic, really. By focusing on healing clients from their disasters, I have gotten the things my parents said I'd get by focusing on myself."

You do not have to work for the poor in order to serve; suffering is everywhere—from skid row to the gleaming high-rises of corporate America—and where there is suffering and need, there is an opportunity to come alive in service. All of us, says meditation teacher and psychotherapist Jack Kornfield, have a "deep longing to give—to give to the earth, to give to others, to give to society." Even in people who don't give, that longing is just waiting to be discovered; failing to find a way to give is "one of the worst human sufferings," he says.

Legal work can honor that impulse, or impede it. When it thwarts the impulse, by marginalizing its importance or failing even to acknowledge its role in the profession (outside of strictly defined pro bono activities), it diminishes the practice.

Halpert is familiar with this diminishment. He recalls the primary message he got in law school, regarding clients: Don't get too involved with them lest it compromise your objectivity. Today he is the senior partner at a four-lawyer personal injury firm in Kalamazoo. Where P.I. lawyers in the area typically have 120 to 150 cases open at a time, each of the partners at Halpert, Weston, Wuori & Sawusch, P.C., handles no more than 20. That's so they can spend a lot of time with their clients—a commitment that often extends for months or even years after a judgment is rendered or a settlement has been reached. "The first obligation of a lawyer with a therapeutic bent," Halpert says, "is to ask the question 'What is in this client's best interest toward peace and happiness and living a meaningful life?'" For Halpert and his partners, answering that question has entailed a level of personal involvement with clients that might seem strange to other lawyers. "Our mission," says Halpert, "is to take care of injured people and help them recover from their accidents—physically, emotionally, psychologically, and financially in a way that allows us to stay in business." To do that, he and his partners have done such things as chauffeur a young burn patient hundreds of miles to a university medical center for treatment when no parent or friend was available to do it; take a leading role in the establishment of a local camp for burned children; spend untold hours on the phone, often on a daily basis, with clients who simply need to express their pain and anger over their predicaments; and finance a trip to Canada to ease the mind of a seriously burned child's mother, who was able to meet there with a group of women who had survived similar childhood injuries to become confident, successful adults.

For Halpert and his partners, such efforts are hardly unusual; they are seen simply as part of what it means to be good and compassionate lawyers. And as far as the last phrase of their mission statement is concerned—"in a way that allows us to stay in business"—they've had little trouble with that. In fact, the firm is known throughout Michigan for the large verdicts and settlements it gets for its clients.

Halpert says he's been accused of arrogance for making choices about what constitutes a meaningful life for his clients. "But I don't make those decisions; I just ask the questions," he says. The point, for him, is that in order to serve your clients' best interests, you *have* to get involved, and—particularly in the case of people who have been badly damaged in accidents—you have to offer them unconditional love, and the sense that you really are committed to their well-being.

"When you're emotionally intimate with a person going through a terrible time and you can make a difference, there's incredible joy in that," says Halpert. "That's the joy that to me makes being a lawyer today worth it."

Like the concept of healing, that of service provides a lens through which to see, and then gauge, the value of your work. By maintaining a service orientation—not just in the sense of giving clients what they want, but also by helping them determine, then get, what they *need* in order to attain some semblance of well-being—you are likely to realize something that too often escapes attention in legal circles: that you have the power, by virtue of your professional and human skills, to lift humanity by moving it incrementally toward greater wholeness. When you can suggest to clients—as Halpert has—that litigation, even if it is likely to result in a huge recovery, is probably *not* in their best interests because of the corrosive effect it will have on family relationships, you have made service your guiding principle. And even though they may reject your advice, you have made the effort to put their best interests first, making service to others more important than self-aggrandizement.

PASSION AND SACRIFICE

Service is a natural expression of who we are. In fact, some psychologists have posited that we have an innate tendency toward altruistic love, and that what we repress, more than sexual impulses or aggression, is affection and openness. If that is true, then the unhappiness among lawyers makes even more sense. What becomes important is finding a way to serve in spite of a culture that has little time for either affection or openness.

In his book *Fire in the Belly*, philosopher Sam Keen says that stress is "a product, not of an excess of fire, but of a deficiency of passion." Lack of passion opens the door to the damaging influences of stress; whereas sufficient passion, given room to express itself, inoculates against it. People who serve others tend to be passionate people. In the needs of others, they see an opportunity for involvement in the very stuff that makes life worthwhile. Such people are open to moments of awe and transcendence in their work because the work is part of a larger calling to be a human being, with all the richness that implies—not a walled-off zone from which spirit and passion have been banished. Halpert, for example, says that working with people in times of crisis is not what he does; it's what he *is*. If he weren't doing it as a lawyer, he would find some other place to do it.

For what may be the purest expression of service in the legal world, it makes sense to look to the world of public-interest law. There, the kinds of sacrifices made are very different from what they are in private practice. Public-interest lawyers typically forgo the opportunity to achieve financial security and are especially vulnerable to the crushing weight of law school debt. But they get something incalculably valuable in return: they work in a world that offers their passion a supportive home, a place where they can let it show and even celebrate it.

University of Georgia law professor Milner Ball suggests that the vitality and excitement he sees in the faces of so many public-interest lawyers has to do with the way they view their relationship to the law. People who, as Ball says, "are free not to be determined by the law so that they can better use it" for some larger good tend to enjoy what they're doing a great deal. They are nourished not by the law, but by their call to service, in which the law is their spear, their plow, their scalpel. It is the means by which they express their passion for helping the poor and disenfranchised. "Richard Posner [of the U.S. Court of Appeals for the 7th Circuit] has referred to the law as 'a humdrum social practice,' and he's right," says Ball.

His point—and perhaps Posner's as well—is that although we can become pious and reverential about it, law is ultimately a tool for use in serving a reality that is beyond the law itself. That reality can be justice, serving the poor, or even protecting property rights, as long as law is seen as the means to achieve goals that enhance our humanity.

Danny Greenberg, director of New York City's 900-lawyer-strong Legal Aid Society, talks about the importance of passion when he addresses groups of public-interest lawyers and students who are considering public-interest careers. "Whatever you do, you should not do this work because it's the most important work," Greenberg says. "Do it because it's what you love doing, because it makes you happy.

"The wonderful thing about this work is that we get to do things that make the dichotomy between being a human being and being a professional as small as it can be," he adds. "You don't have to do something outside this work to fulfill your human goals. That's why the idea that this is a sacrifice is nonsense. It is a luxury to be able to do what you care about and get paid for it."

Greenberg says that when he talks to lawyers in firms, he finds that most of them use language that says, at best, that they're involved in an intellectual endeavor that has little relation to who they are as people. At worst it is antithetical to who they feel they want to be. "But what are the frustrations of public-interest people?" he asks. "That they can't do as much as they'd like to be consistent with who they are as people. But they spend their days reinforcing what they want to be rather than going counter to it."

SERVING OTHERS

Again, working for the poor is not the only way to minimize the gap between being a lawyer and being human (or, perhaps more accurately, to make clear how illusory that gap is), but it is probably most obvious in that setting. Maybe that is because the act of helping another human being who might not otherwise find help is such a transparently worthwhile way to use a law degree. Endeavors such as defending a nursing home in a negligence suit or handling a corporate buyout can feel less clear-cut.

But that may simply reflect a failure of imagination on the part of the legal profession, which seems often to have lost any notion of what, if anything, it is trying to serve. If the ultimate goal is to serve something larger than any single client's financial interests (though that, too, must be a consideration), if it is to serve humanity by using the legal tools and remedies available to mend relationships and ease social stress, then there is no reason that the lawyer who represents the nursing home or the corporation should not be seen—or should not see himself—as walking the path of service.

For Houston criminal defense lawyer Sam Guiberson, the act of putting yourself out on another's behalf has a way of transmuting what would otherwise be mundane legal work into something very special.

"The opportunity to turn the dross of routine law practice into something that reinforces your humanity is what you wait for," says Guiberson. "And this profession gives you that opportunity if you're strong enough within to recognize it when it's upon you and then take it. In that commitment of self, you find the true reward for what we do."

Some years ago, Guiberson volunteered to help with the defense of environmentalist Dave Foreman, whose "eco-terrorism" trial ultimately ended in a plea bargain. Five years later, only weeks after the court allowed Foreman's felony plea to be withdrawn for a misdemeanor offense, Foreman invited Guiberson and his wife and son to his fiftieth birthday party. There, in front of a gathering of some of the country's most renowned environmentalists, Foreman thanked Guiberson for the help he'd given him. "Instead of applause, Dave's friends and colleagues responded with an ovation of wolf howls," Guiberson recalls.

"Despite all the frustration, conflicts, and near financial ruin my volunteer efforts had brought my way, Dave's gratitude, the appreciation of his friends to whom he means so much, and the knowledge that I had helped this environmental advocate continue his work amounted to a moving testimonial for me to the truth that when we give of ourselves, we really help ourselves. When I wonder whether my work has made any difference to anyone, I just return to that remembrance of a criminal defense lawyer being serenaded by wolves."

The Man in the Tattered Suit

Michael Gergely's first boss out of law school in the mid-1960s was Justice Thomas Kavanagh of the Michigan Court of Appeals, who made a strong impression on his young clerk. "He told me that the practice of law is not a business; it's a profession," says Gergely, who now practices law with his two sons and daughter near Kalamazoo. "And he said that finances are not the bottom line; service is."

Gergely believed him, but what he refers to as the most focused and dramatic awareness of what Kavanagh really meant came to him one evening in the early 1970s.

That evening after a full day's work, he was getting ready to leave the office and go home to his wife and children when a disheveled, aimless-looking stranger walked in.

The man sat down, and Gergely asked what he could do for him. The man said he needed help and began to talk. And talk. After a while, not really seeing much of a point to the man's monologue, Gergely became anxious. His wife, Maureen, had made one of his favorite dishes, chicken soup, and he couldn't wait to get started on a hot bowl. At this point, his visitor was talking about the various kinds of lawsuits he thought he might file. But it was going nowhere. Gergely started thinking about how to get rid of him. He recalls what happened next.

"At that instant, I turned to my right, and my eyes fell on a plaque that I have on my wall. It's from the Book of Matthew. It says, 'In as much as ye have done it unto one of the least of these my brethren, ye have done it unto me.' My first reaction was, OK, I am going to be the big person, the charitable person. And as I was turning to look back at the individual, in a millisecond everything changed, and I thought, I'm going to see Christ in this person.

"What I realized then was that I wasn't doing this man a favor; he was helping me by letting me do what I was supposed to be doing in my law office. I was supposed to be serving people, especially the least of my brethren. I forgot about getting home to dinner, and I realized how important that person was. I talked to him for another hour, until he got tired and thanked me and left. I had suggested what he might want to do, but it turned out that he just wanted someone to listen to his problems."

Since then, Gergely has never charged anyone to come in and talk, and he has learned a lesson that has made him a very successful lawyer. "If you treat people right, well, let me put it this way: I have never wanted for clients, and our phones ring off the hook."

Freeing the Helping Heart

In every tradition that emphasizes the importance of the inner life, compassion and service are held up as preeminent virtues. Those who, through the ages, have been revered for their wisdom and empathy—the Gandhis and the Martin Luther Kings of this world, to name but two recent examples—have often been people who believed that the very purpose of life is to be of service to others.

Today's lawyers, being overwhelmingly inclined to minimize the importance of their inner experience, are more apt to see personal enrichment as their purpose, at least in their professional lives. They miss out on the opportunity that Guiberson talks about, to turn the dross of routine legal practice into something that reinforces their humanity ("the

Exercise: At Your Service

> Freely giving your time and energy to others will repay you tenfold. You might consider looking for opportunities each week (or even every day) to perform random, anonymous acts of kindness. It's the holding of doors for others, picking up what someone else dropped, helping an elderly person across the street, or simply offering an encouraging smile that eventually help us to dissolve the boundaries that keep us feeling separate from one another. It will make you feel better and may come to have an impact on the way you practice law.

true reward for what we do"). Why? Because they overwhelmingly lack the inner strength "to recognize the opportunity when it's upon them." This is the great challenge facing much of the legal profession—to once again find the path of service as it leads through every area of the law, and to cultivate an awareness of the opportunities it presents for serving humanity at the individual, communal, and global levels.

Although bar associations have not necessarily made their members' emotional and spiritual well-being their highest priority when encouraging them to do a minimum amount of pro bono work, their advice is sound. And law firms that support pro bono activities, making concessions so that hourly billing requirements do not make such work impossible, may be doing more for their attorneys than they realize, by helping them along a professional path that enhances the potential for satisfaction. After all, satisfied lawyers are healthier, more effective, and productive lawyers.

TRANSFORMING YOUR PRACTICE

In service to others, we learn who we really are. Because there is no lack of suffering in the world, either in the ghetto, in more advantaged neighborhoods, or in the worlds of business and finance, opportunities to serve are never far away.

But service is a mind-set, an orientation that sees the world and one's place in it in a particular way. Until you see it that way—that is, as an expression of a deep need to help—the world of work will offer you few chances to express a yearning that is all too easy to ignore, and fulfillment may prove to be elusive.

Here are some suggestions for bringing the concept of service into your law practice:

- In working with a client, try consciously reframing your role by deciding that your primary goal is to serve the whole person.
- Imagine this: you are sitting before a toolbox in which all of your skills—legal and personal—are neatly arrayed. Try to imagine what you might be able to do with those skills to serve clients, the community, and humankind.
- In some way, acknowledge each client's pain, and let yourself care.
- Ask yourself these questions:
  Have I found something or someone to serve in my work?
  What outlet do I have for my need to be of service?
  If I really care about my clients, do I allow myself to show it?
  How might I bring more caring to my practice?
  What good do I have the power to accomplish?

PART THREE

REDRAWING
THE MAP

We shall not cease from exploration
And the end of all our exploring
Will be to arrive where we started
And know the place for the first time.

—T.S. Eliot, "Little Gidding"

CHAPTER TEN

PRACTICING INTEGRATIVE LAW

If you think that you can think about a thing inextricably attached to something else without thinking of the thing which it is attached to, then you have a legal mind.

—Thomas Reed Powell

Idolatry means the worship of a part of the universe as if it were the whole. . . . In terms of assessing human beings, idolatry is the isolation of a part of the talents of human beings, the IQ, as if it were the whole of the human being.

—Rabbi Harold Schulweis

WHAT MOST OF THE PEOPLE profiled in the previous seven chapters have in common is that they are part of a growing number of lawyers who have begun taking what may best be described as an integrative approach to law practice. Whether they refer to themselves as holistic lawyers, integrative lawyers, or conscious lawyers—or prefer no label at all—they are talking about much the same thing: an orientation toward law practice that shuns the rancor and blood-letting of litigation when-ever possible; seeks to identify the roots of conflict without assigning blame; encourages clients to accept responsibility for their problems and to recognize their opponents' humanity; and sees in every conflict an opportunity for both client and lawyer to let go of judgment, anger, and bias and to grow as human beings.

In order to do this, lawyers who practice holistically set as their goal not only to resolve conflicts, but also to heal the rifts that keep people in pain and denial. Some of them eschew litigation entirely, while others will go to court under certain circumstances.

In contrast to the traditional legal model, the holistic model is about relieving suffering. Another difference is in the very concept of relief, which is traditionally understood in the *Black's Law Dictionary* sense as "the assistance, redress, or benefit which a complainant seeks at the hands of a court. . . . " Monetary awards, injunctions, or the rescission of a contract are, for the holistic attorney, only part of the solution, often the least important part. They may, in a sense, "fix" the problem, but they do little to address the underlying causes, or the pain and disori-entation that the client may continue to feel. To facilitate a process by which the client can truly become whole again, other kinds of relief must also be made available, kinds that are limited only by the participants' imagination and vision. Some of the ingredients that holistic lawyers might employ in order to really relieve suffering are helping the client to let go of anger, helping to foster forgiveness, encouraging the recogni-tion of one's part in a dispute, and supporting the recognition of others' perspectives. All of this can be, and ideally is, empowering for the cli-ent, and gaining a sense of power—of potency in the world—can itself restore a sense of integration and well-being.

Holistic lawyers practice in a wide variety of settings, in big cities and small towns, in government and corporate law departments; they do civil rights work and family law, employment law and transactional law; they are prosecutors and public defenders.

It is probably safe to say that most holistic lawyers see nothing oxy-moronic in the use of the words "joy" and "law practice" in the same sentence. That's largely because they make a determined effort *not* to separate their personal and professional lives; it's part of the holistic out-look—work and nonwork are both part of the unity that is each person, and that unity is in turn part of larger unities, including family, the community, and, ultimately, the universe. That's certainly true of the following three lawyers, each of whom abandoned a traditional legal practice in favor of more integrative approaches.

Delores Cordell

In 1977, Delores Cordell was, by all outward appearances, leading an enviable life. "I had become a lawyer, a home owner, and a mother and started working at a law firm all within fourteen months," she says. Off and running, she made partner as soon as it was possible and earned good money. "Everyone looked at me and said, 'She's got it all.'"

A successful litigator, she kept running, without a vacation, for fourteen years, until she got what she calls "the proverbial kick in the ass." Her fourteen-year-old son fell into a suicidal depression, and her marriage hit the rocks. She stood at a crossroads. One way led to the Band-Aid approach—buy the best psychological help available and keep right on living like the "adrenaline junkie" she was. The alternative was to shake the monkey off her back and do some real soul-searching.

For Cordell, it was an easy call. She decided to leave the marriage and move from Los Angeles to Marin County north of San Francisco, where she planned to wait tables if that's what it took to find a better, saner life for herself and her two children. That turned out not to be necessary, as her law partners had a delightfully surprising reaction to her plans: they suggested she open a San Francisco office.

"I've really come to believe in miracles," she says. "After that, I sold my house in a lousy market in four weeks with 20 percent down and no contingency. It was like I just got on a wave and rode it. Now I've been here for three and a half years, doing nothing but employment law (she had previously had a more varied litigation practice). And I keep getting more excited by the subject matter of what I'm doing, because it's about work. That's what human beings do—spend time with family and work—and relationships in the workplace are critical to our lives."

Cordell found that the process of changing her life began to express itself in her law practice and in her feelings about the work. A lawyer who once did nothing but adversarial work, she now sees herself mainly as a counselor and a guide to her employer-clients. "I've become a much better lawyer through this," she says. "I'm much closer with clients than I ever was, and it's not just about making money anymore. It's become much more about my service, my ministry in the world." What gives her the greatest pleasure, she says, is "bringing truth to a really convoluted, ugly legal situation. A lot of times, no one is speaking the truth about what is going on. When I can provide that to a client, it's really an ecstatic experience."

True to the holistic model, she also has found that broadening the framework in which she sees her work adds a new dimension to it and makes it more fulfilling. "I know I can prevent clients from being sued," she says. "I know I can do it. And it's a great pleasure knowing the money I'm going to save them will go into higher salaries, vacations, and new equipment. Avoiding problems ultimately makes the workplace a better place for everyone."

Above all, Cordell has learned to trust, both in the plenitude of the universe, where fear of deprivation no longer keeps her running, and in her own intuition. "For years, I would practice law and every few months I'd say, 'Darn! I knew I should have done *x*.' Now I'll sometimes open my mouth and something comes out that, honest to God, I don't know where it's come from, and it's right on the mark. When I have a gut reaction, I let it out. In the past, I'd ignore them.

"The thing is," she says, "I really needed to develop my own way of being a lawyer."

Carroll Straus

Carroll Straus was also due for a change of approach, although that wasn't clear to her in November 1991, when she boarded a plane to Chicago, where her mother was gravely ill. Although she had not been very close to her, Straus felt strongly that her mother shouldn't be allowed to die alone. Being with her when she died changed Straus.

"It was very similar to what people report after a near-death experience," she says. "I came away with no fear of death and a totally changed outlook on life. I saw love as the answer—and all that mushy stuff. I even cried every time I thought of it. People thought I was crazy, and so did I, but there was no arguing with the fact that it changed me." And the change in Straus's consciousness transformed Straus the lawyer.

"After that, I couldn't go back and do what I'd done—put on my armor and go into battle. I *couldn't* do it. I thought I'd be a freelance writer; that's how certain I was. But that wasn't going to work out. Finally it dawned on me that I was, by inclination if not by training, a healer, and I realized that it was time to bring the law and healing together."

Achieving a result that is healing sometimes comes about almost accidentally for Straus, who practices on her own in Orange County, California. "I'll just do what looks, sounds, and feels right to me, and often it works," she says. Some time ago, for example, she represented a Mexican family who had been rear-ended in their Ford Pinto by an uninsured and drugged-out driver. Thankfully, they were spared the fate of certain other rear-ended Pinto drivers, but damage was done. "I had him agree to make installment payments and apologize to my clients. Oddly, he kept making the payments long after he was required to. I think it must have been healing for him to do that."

Much of Straus's work is generated by her Web page, on which she bills herself as an attorney-healer. She's attracted an eclectic range of cases. Ultimately, her goal is to stop representing people in the traditional way—something she hasn't yet achieved due to financial realities—and instead coach them through, or around, the legal system.

Alice Best

For Alice Best, the movement toward holistic practice began when her two best friends died within two years of each other. "That got me onto the spiritual path," she says. "It made me pause for a while and say, 'Something is going on here.' Then I got back into the fray." But she never entirely lost the sense that life was trying to tell her something.

Eventually she felt the pull toward holistic law. Today she has a family law practice in the Ft. Lauderdale office of the 100-lawyer firm of Becker & Poliakoff. "The spiritual side of things puts everything back in perspective," she says. "You realize there's a reason for things.

"I've come to look at things so differently. Now when I counsel clients, I'll say, 'This chapter was written before you were married; perhaps before you were born, and no amount of crying will change it. But there was a purpose for your marriage; maybe it was to have your children. Look how great they are! Now the question is, Can you go on with your life?' They say yes, and we find a way for them to do that." Best doesn't talk that way to everyone, though, only to clients who she senses will be open to it. If, for example, she is able to find out what a client enjoys reading, she usually can tell whether the person will respond well to her spiritual analyses. A surprising number are open to it.

Even before her friends' deaths, Best wasn't satisfied with law practice. "I had wanted to be a lawyer so badly, and when I became one, my feeling was, 'This is it?' I loved dealing with the people, but not with the lawyers and judges and all the games. Now it's gotten to the point where, by practicing holistically, I no longer dislike my career. I can say I do this, it's my profession, but I do it *this* way. I do go to court, unlike some holistic lawyers. But if someone wants to settle and offers less than what my client can get going into court blind, I'm not stupid. I'll go."

One place her holistic perspective comes into play, says Best, is in the kind of case in which a client wants to sue her husband, his family, their corporation, and everyone else she can cast the legal net around. "Some lawyers will jump right into it," she says. "I won't. I'll ask, 'What's going to happen down the road? What's your relationship with your in-laws? What's your children's relationship with them? What is this going to do to you and the people you care about in the long run?' I make them look at what's going to happen first."

Previously a solo practitioner, Best made it clear when she interviewed with Becker & Poliakoff that she had a rather unusual perspective on the law. And she credits the firm for their open-mindedness in hiring her and being willing to mention her membership in the International Alliance of Holistic Lawyers (see box, p. 134) in her profile on their Web site. She's up front with clients too. "I tell them that we'll try to reach a settlement first, that I litigate only if absolutely necessary, that I'll do all I can to save them the most money possible and create the least amount of stress in their lives. I guess my greatest compliment so far is that I get referrals from one of my client's exes."

Because Best makes no attempt to hide her true legal colors, everyone in the office knows what she's about. And many have expressed interest. In fact, when she regularly goes to lunch with a group of eight colleagues, she says, "nine out of ten times, the conversation turns to holistic and spiritual concerns."

A FOCUS ON THE FUTURE

Both holistic law in general and the dispute-resolution process that most holistic lawyers favor—mediation—tend to be more future-oriented than traditional legal approaches. Litigation looks to right a past wrong, while holistic law and mediation also seek a resolution that addresses the desire for harmony in the future.

Vermont lawyer William van Zyverden, who coined the term "holistic law," describes his future-oriented approach allegorically: "You've just been shot with an arrow. What are you going to do first? Go after the person who shot you? You'll probably bleed to death. Or will you heal the wound first and then figure out what to do? It doesn't mean you won't eventually go after the other person, but it probably shouldn't be the first thing you do. And if you just work on blaming the other person, you won't heal the wound. Until you take responsibility for standing in front of the target, it will be your natural inclination to do it again."

Van Zyverden says that rather than advocate for a client's anger ("when a lawyer does that, he serves no one"), a lawyer should zealously advocate for "the whole picture, and not just the present picture, but also the future picture, because sometimes the lawyer knows what is going to happen. He may know the whole scenario from experience. He may know the other lawyer, too. It may just be a matter of saying, 'Here's the likely picture; is this the road you want to go down?'"

Like many other holistic lawyers, van Zyverden strives to take blame out of the equation when he's working with a client. "I've come to see that everything is dependent on what preceded it," he says. "There isn't a thing, a thought, a feeling, or a behavior that doesn't have a history in front of it. When you start to see situations that way, then blame goes right out of the picture. There may be all kinds of places where your client could have intervened, and things might have gone differently, and it's important that she take some responsibility for things happening the way they did. Once she does, then it becomes much easier to work with the other side.

"When a client comes in and says, 'This keeps happening to me,' a lawyer should say, 'Of course it happens over and over again. When are you going to see that if you proceed in the same way over and over again, you'll never get out of the loop?' But are we taught to say that? No. We're taught to defend clients against things. But people keep marrying the same person over and over, walking down the same dark alley over and over, and so on. Then they ask, 'Why is this happening to me?' And who better to point that out than the lawyer, who has seen it over and over again? It's a matter of just pointing out something you've seen in your experience."

Although many lawyers assume that clients are loath to be told such things, van Zyverden says they appreciate the insights. "It's like a light goes on," he says. "They'll often say, 'You know, I've never thought of it that way.' And the fact that I approach things that way doesn't mean that I won't champion their cause. That's part of the whole. What it means is that I include helping to heal their suffering in what I do as a lawyer."

Sometimes going after the other side is integral to the client's belief system (and the lawyer is obliged to determine what that belief system is, rather than assuming he knows). Van Zyverden offers a simple landlord-tenant case that he handled as an example. "The client said the landlords had done all sorts of nasty things, and she wanted money from them," he recalls. "I asked her how much she wanted to stay in the relationship.

"She told me she wanted out of it. So, I said, 'OK, do you believe that suing them will free you of the relationship or drag it out?' She said, 'They owe me big-time, and it's the only way I'll get it.' So I asked her if she'd feel better if she gets the money or if she gets them out of her life. She said she never wanted to see them again, and I asked what if she never gets the money. She said, 'I want the money,' and I asked her if she was sure and suggested that she think about it for a while. We had the time; the statute had a couple of years to run. I told her to try just getting out and seeing how she felt about it.

"I saw her again after a while. She said, 'Boy, am I glad I'm free of them.' So I asked her what about the money, and she said, 'Who cares?' The point of this is that sometimes you have to ask clients the questions that lead to healing, or at least get them to consider what might be healing for them." One way of doing this, van Zyverden says, comes from his previous career in sales. "A standard thing to do when someone doesn't want to buy is to ask, 'If I can provide you with x, y, or z, would that solve your problem?' I do the same thing with clients. I need to ask, 'What would make you whole again? What would restore you?'

"If the client says, 'I need to win this lawsuit. I need some money,' then there needs to be more investigating done. You don't know if it's genuine or if it's just being said. Lawyers need to be open to hearing and feeling the genuineness of the client's answers. I also have to keep in mind that neither the client nor I can know the full palette of possibilities. It's part of the teamwork. If you give the client a, b, and c options, then those are just your own options. Instead, you have to be open to something you never considered."

HOLISTIC LITIGATION

Thomas Porter, who launched a mediation practice after twenty-five years as a litigator in Boston, feels strongly that mediation should be the primary response to conflict transformation, and that litigation should be used only as a backup or in certain rare instances when principles of great importance require adjudication.

Porter, who is involved with a local group called Lawyers with a Holistic Approach, does not see the ultimate cessation of litigation as a desirable goal; he considers it an appropriate *second-line* choice for resolving disputes. "If the adversarial approach is used only when mediation is not appropriate," he says, "then the role of the lawyer can be seen to be not only as an advocate—which is a very noble thing, particularly when you advocate for people's relationships—but, also, I think, as a peacemaker. We need a paradigm to balance out adversarial ethics because they've become so dominant. Then you would constantly rub together your roles as a peacemaker and as an adversary. They're not always in harmony, but out of this tension you can create something very creative."

Litigation remains an effective tool when it is used consciously and with respect for the humanity of the other side. Unfortunately, van Zyverden points out, lawyers tend to spend half their time tearing down the other side, leaving only the other half to prepare the theme of the case. "I spend 100 percent of my time preparing my case," he says. "But we were all taught in law school and in CLEs all about humiliating witnesses, discrediting them, getting information on them, and so on. I don't go to those CLEs anymore. I want to spend my time not learning how to win, but how to help people."

Sylvia Clute, a member of the van Zyverden-founded International Alliance of Holistic Lawyers, spent so many years as a tough and successful trial lawyer in Richmond, Virginia, that easing herself into a more holistic practice has taken some doing. A trial lawyer for more than twenty years, she remembers the day back in moot court at Boston University Law School when she admitted that her opponent's argument had some merit. "I was told that was wrong, that I should go for the jugular and never concede anything," she recalls. "So I went out into the world under that assumption, and I established myself and did very well."

But Clute's practice was changed by the spiritual/self-help classic *A Course in Miracles*, as well as by readings in ancient spiritual wisdom and the study of quantum physics. Today she holds that separation is an illusion, and she says it has become clear to her that when people hurt each other, they are literally hurting themselves as well.

"All of our tort laws—and I've done a lot of tort work—are based on the concept of separation. If I drive down the street and you run into me, I have nothing to do with that. But the new science says we're all involved in everything. I didn't have to be there. Now, what does that do to the last clear chance doctrine (which holds that if a party has the last

 The International Alliance of Holistic Lawyers

If you're thinking of—or fantasizing about—stepping off the edge of the known legal universe, you ought to be aware that others have done it before you. Many of them are members of the International Alliance of Holistic Lawyers, founded in 1991 by William van Zyverden.

Based at the Holistic Justice Center in Middlebury, Vermont, the Alliance was created to support lawyers who share van Zyverden's concerns about the state of the legal profession. Today the organization serves as an umbrella for lawyers who hold a variety of alternative visions but are nonetheless like-minded. Most eschew narrow legalistic thinking and approaches that separate people from one another and from their own best instincts, and believe that every lawyer and client must operate with the sense of responsibility that comes from knowing that they are part of a larger whole. IAHL members come from all parts of the country and represent a broad variety of practice settings in both the private and government sectors, and include corporate, family, criminal, employment, and civil rights lawyers, among others.

Members find support through the IAHL in a variety of ways, including a quarterly newsletter, regular meetings of regional chapters, an annual conference, and numerous informal networks that the Alliance has spawned. The same goes for law students, who can join the Alliance and explore alternative career paths through meetings of law school-based chapters nationwide.

Truly an international organization, the IAHL has members from more than twenty countries, and new members are automatically registered with the International Holistic Lawyer Referral Service. They receive referrals from the IAHL when members of the public contact the organization to find a holistic lawyer in their area.

For more information on the IAHL, contact:
International Alliance of Holistic Lawyers
6212 OC Hester Road
Holly Springs, NC 27540
Fax: (919) 882-8881
E-mail: info@iahl.org
www.iahl.org

clear chance to get out of a situation, the other party is absolved of legal negligence)? Under quantum physics, everyone has the last clear chance. I think we have to redefine our concept of responsibility to one another. Vengeance is not working out, and this is why."

Within her general civil litigation practice, Clute has developed a specialty that she says allows her to use litigation holistically as a healing tool. It is in the area known as sexual torts, where Clute represents people who have been sexually abused, some as children by trusted adults, and others as adults by trusted professionals, usually doctors. "These are situations when a person in a position of trust took their power away," she says. "I find that the courtroom can be a great place to reempower them, as long as they have no attachment to the outcome. It allows you to use all the spiritual tools, such as being in the moment and validating their experience. These are really spiritual injuries that I'm talking about, and it is the process, not the result, that can be healing."

THE ART OF MEDIATION

Many lawyers with a holistic orientation see mediation as their first-line choice for resolving disputes because they tend to be especially aware of their clients *in relationship*, and in mediation, relationships take center stage. They're what the process is about. It's not about winning, nor is it about revenge. And if it begins with each side intent on assigning blame, a skilled mediator will find a way to get beyond that surface motivation to what lies beneath.

Porter points out that as we have become increasingly legalistic in our relationships—defining them in ever-greater detail—we have often ignored the *spirit* of the relationship. Mediation can provide a forum for exploring that spirit and for tapping into its potential for personal and even social transformation.

The processes of litigation and mediation are fundamentally different on every level, including the inner level—the level of being—for both the client and the lawyer. Santa Monica mediator Kenneth Cloke calls it "the difference between justice being pronounced from outside, and the feeling in both parties that a given result is fair." Cloke points out that mediation works fundamentally by taking people not *out* of themselves into some objective space, but *into* a mutually subjective space—that is, into each person's story. With the help of a skilled mediator, the process of dipping into each person's story often leads to an opportunity that is rarely presented in court, by which each party is able to witness the other person's essential humanity. This can have a powerfully healing effect, as perceived differences melt away or are accepted as non-threatening parts of who the other is.

For the lawyer, working as a mediator calls on a whole range of skills and sensitivities thought to have little relevance to the litigator's art. These skills require sensitivity to the very human issues for which litigation, by virtue of its procedural complexity and rigidity, seems to have less room (even if the enlightened litigator knows otherwise). Because the participants move toward a resolution that feels right for them, rather than something imposed upon them by a court or through settlement, it will be their personalities, temperaments, emotional makeup, and personal histories that underlie their choices. Being a good mediator means knowing something about forgiveness. It means being able to put one's own beliefs and convictions aside and allow someone else's to be more important. It means being sensitive to what people need at a given moment in their lives in order to heal and how the process can be advanced through mediation.

Mediation calls on the lawyer as human *being* in a much more obvious way than litigation does. Skill is crucial, but it's not enough. A mediator must have presence as well. Who he *is*—above and beyond what he does—is absolutely critical. If he cannot put his ego aside long enough to allow the opposing parties' own hopes, dreams, and yearnings to fill the room, he will not gain their trust, nor will he succeed at achieving the best result possible. Mediators are rewarded for attaining what the poet John Keats called "negative capability," the capacity to be "in uncertainties, mysteries, doubts, without any irritable reaching after fact and reason." When they have this mind-set, they allow people to be who they are without any need to judge or change them. They can then search for a solution that is consistent with the meaning *they* find in the dispute rather than what the lawyer thinks is most appropriate.

Healing Relationships

Seeing this revelatory process blossom is something that lawyer-mediator Forrest Mosten finds deeply moving. Of hundreds of examples he could call on, he cites a mediation he did for a rock band that was quite well known in the 1960s. All these years later, with a few of them suffering from age-related health problems, they became embroiled in litigation over royalties after some of their old songs were republished on a CD. In addition, several members had formed new bands, each performing under the old band's name. It wasn't clear who should have the rights to use the name. "You could just watch them as they began replaying postpubescent conflicts about romantic entanglements and choices of music," Mosten says.

"At the end of a two-day mediation, one band member came into the office with the patent on the name and handed it over to another member. Then he gave a talk about how he'd grown up with these people, how they were part of his life, and said that he only wished them well. His own sadness was palpable. He only wished they could start again. They hugged each other, and the feeling in the room was incredible."

Two Types of Mediation

As mediation has become ever more popular as a dispute-resolution technique, particularly in the courts and in private business, there has been an increasing tendency to see it as an efficient settlement tool, a way of simply disposing of cases. The emphasis most often is on efficiency and cost saving. Call that "problem-solving mediation."

Another kind of mediation—one that harks back to the original purpose of the process—is one that emphasizes its transformative potential. "I sometimes ask people what the difference is between an iceberg and a river," says Ken Cloke. "They're both water, but one is frozen and one is flowing. When you get the energy flowing, you open up possibilities for transformation—because you're not taking people to places other than their true center."

Law professors Robert Baruch Bush and Joseph P. Folger, authors of *The Promise of Mediation*, explain that transformative mediation has an altogether different set of priorities from the problem-solving type. It allows for the possibility, to use their definition, of a "change or refinement in the consciousness and character" of the disputants. The tools the transformative mediator uses to maximize the chances of bringing about such a change include:

- fostering empowerment—restoring to people the sense of their own value, strength, and ability to handle their own problems

- simultaneously fostering a capacity for recognition—the ability to acknowledge and feel empathy for others' problems
- helping the parties "recognize and exploit the opportunities for moral growth inherently presented in conflict"

Transformative mediation is about facilitating change in *people*, rather than just situations. In fact, a mediator working with this model may point out to the parties that settlement is but one possible outcome, and that even without settlement, there is much to be gained, and learned, from the process.

Seeing conflict as "a field full of opportunities for empowerment and recognition," Bush and Folger call for expanding the use of transformative mediation—especially as they see our culture moving away from an individualist perspective toward a relational worldview that stresses the importance of integrating individuality and connectedness, cultivating concern for others, and empathy. It is this worldview, they point out, that the transformative approach to mediation flows from and expresses.

Viewed in this light, dispute resolution is an adjunct to a larger project: the reinstatement of relationship—rather than individuality—as the primary unit of spirit in our world. Transformative mediation—with its emphasis on empowerment and recognition and its attempt to cultivate compassionate strength—is a model that is highly amenable to the kind of spiritual insights from which acts of protracted warfare (i.e., traditional litigation) will shut you off. These include the realization that:

- People are essentially good and, when they feel safe enough to express their real feelings and needs, have a deep impulse toward making things right and healing their relationships.
- Parties that feel empowered to work out their own solutions tend to gravitate toward what they both feel to be just.
- Judgment is destructive; it closes the heart and so inhibits resolution and the possibility of transformation.
- All people are connected, and ego, poor communication, fear, and confusion foster the illusion of separateness.

One crucial distinction between litigation and mediation is the degree to which mediation allows for consideration not only of the parties' actions (their outer lives) but also their beliefs, feelings, and motivations (their inner lives). The legal world's overemphasis on the outer world notwithstanding, we all operate in both spheres. This is a major reason why people with a holistic view of life tend to be drawn to the meditative process. A client's feelings and beliefs don't tend to count for much in a courtroom, and that limits the range of solutions available to litigants.

Mediation empowers clients by allowing them to find their own solutions to problems. With the help of a skilled neutral party, they can think and feel and discuss their way along their own road to restitution and accountability.

"Where I am now is a function of how I used mediation," says Lise Luttgens, who is chief operating officer of Children's Hospital Los Angeles, and whose divorce Mosten mediated in 1995. Paradoxically, one of the ways Luttgens was able to use the process—which in her case was protracted and particularly painful—was in learning to relinquish control, something she had always found extremely hard to do. "It wasn't fun for me. It made me angry, but it was transformational for me to be able to give up my need to have everything the way I wanted it to be. I gave that control to the mediator."

OTHER ALTERNATIVES

Among people who have decided that practicing law in the usual way is no longer an option, a variety of new approaches have taken hold. It's a trend you can expect to see grow as more of these alternatives demonstrate their viability, both economically and as satisfying career choices. The following two variations on a mediative theme represent the kinds of success stories that can only give heart to lawyers who love helping people solve their problems but who suffer because the profession rewards combative, time-consuming, disempowering, and ultimately counterproductive methods of getting the job done.

The Unbundled Divorce

The six lawyers at Divorce Helpline in Santa Cruz, California, came together in 1990 to offer a humane alternative to litigation in times of crisis. Witnesses to the human wreckage that results when anger and recrimination set the tone for divorce, they shared a belief that the adversarial system was harming far more families than it helped.

With two strict rules underlying all that they do—they will not go to court, nor will they ever take sides in a case—Divorce Helpline attorneys offer such services as consultation, mediation, document drafting, and settlement conferencing. They put a premium on clients' controlling their own cases, rather than turning them over to their lawyers or to a judge. For this reason, they offer their services unbundled; that is, clients can buy any single service or combination of services they feel would meet their needs.

Divorce Helpline has found a large and growing market for its services—now about 3,500 people a year. About half of those clients come into the firm's office; the other half obtain the same services—including mediation—over the phone. Only 5 percent of the firm's clients ever end up in court.

"Our approach is for the whole family," says founding partner Anne Lober. "We always work for cooperative settlements." Having defined their practice as one in which trial is not an option, Lober says she and her partners have had to become extremely imaginative and open to possibilities that will keep their clients out of court.

Lober describes the traditional approach to handling divorces as "two guys fighting in the absence of the reality of your life." Instead of going that route, Lober and her colleagues let clients make their own decisions using the skills they already have, "just as they did when they decided to build a house or to have children or to take a vacation."

For Lober, work is her calling, not just a job. "Whether or not clients are transformed by the process, it's transforming for me," she says. On a very personal level, the process has freed her from thought patterns she absorbed early in life. "I come from a very judgmental family," she says. "But I'm incapable now of the kind of side-taking that most of us take for granted in our families and in our lives."

When she now looks at lawyers engaged in adversarial solutions to clients' problems, she sees "a superficial analysis of things. Here you have a client who is angry at her husband, and you adopt her position, when if you met the husband in another setting, you may very well have liked him. Or, if he had walked through your door first, you would have taken his side. It's so arbitrary." This becomes unhealthy for lawyers, Lober says, because they wind up taking on their clients' anger. "Taking on anger is extremely unhealthy, and the fact that lawyers are constantly doing it is a big part of why we're such an unhappy profession."

Collaborative Law

Another variation on the mediation theme is collaborative law, an idea that came to then-trial lawyer Stuart Webb in the late 1980s. "In order for me to be in a working relationship with my clients where we could work things out with another lawyer and his or her client, the whole idea of going to court had to go," he recalls. The more Webb thought about this idea, he says, the more profound it became, even though it required him to reassess and replace much of what he had learned.

Webb's evolution from trial work to a practice in which court battles have no place started with a personal crisis. "In the late '60s, I had a realization that I was totally, absolutely outer directed," he says. "I had no sense of who I was. I felt like a chameleon. It was a terribly scary realization that I had no sense of an inside."

It was out of his search for an "inside" that collaborative law was eventually born. It is a process that blends the principles of mediation with what is called a four-way meeting, which brings lawyers and clients together around a table to try to solve a problem. Webb says he has learned a lot about the role of the "inner lawyer" from friends and acquaintances in the mediation community, enabling him to drop a lot of the "outer learning" he says he no longer needs.

Since 1990, when the Collaborative Law Institute was founded in Minneapolis as a nonprofit umbrella group for collaborative lawyers, the number of practitioners in the Twin Cities who do collaborative family law has grown to more than forty. But Webb does not work only with lawyers in the collaborative law network. He also calls on traditional lawyers and asks them if they're open to doing collaborative work in a particular case. Sometimes they are.

The idea has spread, and there are lawyers practicing collaborative law in at least six other cities. Webb is frequently invited by groups around the country to come out and explain the process.

Like family mediation, there is no formal discovery in collaborative law. All information on assets and income is shared. Also like mediation, the collaborative process often leads to results that are unheard of in a court of law. One of Webb's favorite stories is of a collaborative case in which the subject of the four-way meeting was child support. "As he was looking at his wife's budget, the husband said, 'Well, you're not going to have enough money. I think I'm going to have to give you a couple hundred more in child support.' There was silence, then the wife said, 'I think I'm supposed to say that.'"

"Now, this wasn't a case where the people were that together, that close, where you would have expected it," Webb says. "But that kind of thing happens all the time. We'll be working with complex issues—say, with a doctor and his wife and four kids and very complicated assets—and as we're reaching an agreement around the table, I'll think to myself, 'There's six weeks in trial that nobody has to go through.'"

For Webb, one of the greatest benefits of the collaborative process is that he has been able to form personal relationships with other lawyers. Where earlier he kept them at a distance, knowing he was likely to be battling it out with them at some point, today he views them as his compatriots.

TRANSFORMING YOUR PRACTICE

Ultimately, practicing holistically is not a matter of what kind of work you do, but rather what the guiding intention behind the work is. If you take the broad view, try not to hurt people, acknowledge your connections to others and the connection between the inner and the outer life, you are a holistic lawyer—no matter what kind of law you practice.

Los Angeles mediator Forrest Mosten emphasizes the importance of being "growth ready," that is, ready to help facilitate personal growth when the opportunity presents itself. This readiness, a hallmark of the holistic approach, is part of what makes it satisfying for lawyers who choose to practice integrative law. For them the goal is to use the law to serve their clients' humanity, rather than allow it to be stifled or undermined. And if their growth-readiness embraces the possibility of their own emotional and moral development, then the gap between the professional and the personal all but disappears.

Here are a few suggestions on how to move toward a more integrative law practice:

- Make it your job to help your client see the larger picture, including how the matter at hand may affect her life one year, five years, or ten years down the line.
- Make a commitment to practicing law from the heart as well as the head.

- Try to look beyond what appear to be separate interests to the common interests that may serve as the basis for reconciliation.
- Try to make your client a partner in his case. Get him involved in the process, and ask him to contribute his thoughts and insights to the process.
- Let yourself show that you care about the client as a human being.
- Commit yourself to *not* taking on and acting out your clients' aggression.
- Consider the possibility that law practice can be a vehicle for personal growth and happiness—both for you and for clients.

CHAPTER ELEVEN

THE NEW CLIENT

Here we stand, confronted by insurmountable opportunities.

—Pogo Possum

CLIENTS ARE CHANGING. And the ways in which they are changing may represent new opportunities for lawyers who are sensitive to the imperatives of the inner life.

One client of an East Coast intellectual property lawyer—an inventor—never visits the lawyer without meditating first in the park across the street from the office. This fascinates the lawyer, who has never met a client like him: his purpose never seems to be to win, and instead he appears to be involved in some other kind of game having to do with deeper concerns, some of which he explains, some of which he doesn't. And although he comes to the lawyer for advice, he makes it very clear that he sees him as a partner.

A Los Angeles woman seeking a divorce impressed her lawyer when she insisted she wanted to take the high road and ask for nothing but child support—even though she had ample evidence to prove that her husband had physically abused her. A practitioner of both martial arts and meditation, she felt herself to be on a spiritual path that obligated her to "bring more love and less rancor into the world."

A family lawyer in Massachusetts has seen a surge in interest in incorporating rituals into her work. When marriages end, for example, clients sometimes ask her to say some words, or a prayer, to acknowledge the significance of the moment.

A New Jersey architect interviewed five different lawyers after he lost most of the function in his left hand in an accident on a job site. He wanted to talk about what would be fair and just in terms of a settlement with the contractor. He was shocked to find that every lawyer he spoke to became bellicose. Each one promised to go after the man tooth and nail, even though the architect had never had a cross word with him during a ten-year working relationship. Stunned by their apparent lack of concern for what made sense to him and would jibe with his personal ethics and values, he found himself frustrated and bewildered.

And Cheryl Conner, associate director of clinical programs at Suffolk University Law School, was deluged with phone calls after she was featured in a *Boston Herald* article on holistic lawyering and its goals. "These were people involved in litigation looking for ways to understand and find meaning in the fact that they had a conflict in their lives," she recalls, "and asking for advice on how to coach their lawyers to make it more meaningful spiritually."

Conner may have run into the tip of a very important iceberg. In his 1996 *Integral Culture Survey: A Study of the Emergence of Transformational Values in America*, sociologist/urban planner Paul H. Ray identified a growing subculture in America that he calls the "Cultural Creatives." He estimates their numbers at 23.6 percent of the population, or 44 million people. Characteristics of the group include high levels of education, a median income of $47,500, and a median age of forty-two. They are seriously concerned with psychology, spiritual life, self-actualization, and self-expression. Values in which Cultural Creatives scored high (compared with "Heartlanders" and "Modernists"—the two other significant subcultures Ray identified) included "want to rebuild neighborhoods/community" (92 percent), "see nature as sacred" (85 percent), "believe in ecological sustainability" (83 percent), and "believe in voluntary simplicity" (79 percent). These are people, Ray writes, "open to innovation in the service of their spiritual values."

It's safe to say a hefty percentage of those 44 million people are going to seek legal help some day. When they do, they will bring a different consciousness to it—suggesting that lawyers may soon have more room

than they have now to try new ways of doing things. In other words, it is likely that this large (and growing) subculture, which embraces "alternative" or "progressive" values, will prefer lawyers whose approach is consistent with their own worldview.

That was certainly true of Judi Neal, a litigant whose "cultural creative" values came smack up against some very unspiritual opponents and, with the help of her lawyers, stood their ground.

A New Client's Approach to Litigation

Of the words used to describe the experience of being a litigant in a high-stakes lawsuit, some don't bear repeating in polite company. Of those that do, some hark back to Ambrose Bierce's definition of litigation in his *Devil's Dictionary* as "a machine which you go into a pig and come out of as a sausage." Others have described it simply as the worst thing they've ever been through.

Judi Neal calls it "one of the most powerful and wonderful spiritual experiences" of her life. When she brought a whistle-blower suit against the giant Honeywell Inc. in 1992—a suit that continued for more than six years—she was unusually well prepared to see it that way.

Now the director of both the Center for University Business Partnerships and the Center for Spirit at Work at the University of New Haven, Neal has a Ph.D. in organizational behavior from Yale University. She worked for Honeywell in the mid-'80s as an organizational consultant at their Joliet, Illinois, ammunition plant. After two years, she was asked to do some team building in the company's ballistics division, where there had been problems with employee morale. It wasn't long before she discovered the reason: workers had been asked to falsify data, passing off defective arms as flawless.

Having previously set up an ethics hot line to corporate counsel, Neal decided it was time to use it herself. Thousands of shredded documents and numerous threats later—and feeling that her life was in danger—she left Illinois and returned to her home state of Connecticut.

After an initial period of unemployment and depression, she began to trust that there was a reason for all that was happening in her life. Then things turned around. She joined the faculty at the University of New Haven and did something she had promised herself she would do while still at Honeywell: "I made a vow to live with integrity, live my principles,

be myself and not live in fear. I realized I could live my spirituality and not be in conflict. I started to be more open about it, and I got incredible support, including research grants. It was like I was finally at home."

Neal began discussing her experience at Honeywell in her classes, hoping to wring some good out of it. "I talked about creating a trusting environment, and I showed them what happens if you don't, and if you take away people's power to solve problems internally." Then, while reading a textbook about whistle-blowing, she discovered the *qui tam* law, and a light went on. "I realized there was a way that I could get justice and make sure they didn't get away with what they had done."

That eventually brought Neal back to Illinois, where she found William Holloway and Michael Leech of the Chicago law firm of Hinshaw & Culbertson. They filed her case one week before the statute of limitations had run. Much to their surprise, Honeywell made no attempt to settle out of court—even in the face of what Neal's team considered to be overwhelming evidence.

By this time, Neal had come to see opportunities for spiritual growth in every part of her life. The lawsuit, though, proved to be an extraordinary test. During her protracted ordeal, she faced diverse humiliations, fearsome attacks on her credibility, and exposure of the most intimate details of her private life. But after a bruising courtroom battle, during which Neal was asked questions about childhood sexual abuse, among other intensely personal matters, a jury found in her favor.

In the end, she was neither traumatized nor numb. Instead, she felt grateful and full of energy. "And it was because of my lawyers," she says. Her lawyers beg to differ, attributing Neal's enthusiasm about the experience entirely to her own worldview. But that just goes to show how much of a collaboration such relationships can be, with each party taking sustenance from the other.

A Collaboration Begins

In truth her lawyers made a huge difference. They didn't scoff at her spirituality; they embraced it. They didn't try to make her conform to their notion of how a client is *supposed* to behave; they appreciated her uniqueness. They didn't dictate to her; they made her a partner in the endeavor, and they learned from her. Leech recalls that he bonded with Neal in a way he had done with few previous clients. "What happens in these situations is that the person will say something in the course of our first conversa-

tion—he or she will express some philosophical or theological viewpoint in an understated way. Then you respond by illustrating familiarity with that reference or perhaps by mentioning what might be a familiar text. Within a few minutes, you both know you have a spiritual side and that it's important enough for you not to keep it hidden all the time."

But with Neal, it was deeper than with previous clients, and Leech quickly understood her need to make the lawsuit an expression of her inner life. "There doesn't seem to be a part of Judi that's compartmentalized or separated from her spiritual life," he says. "She's consistently in touch with that part of herself."

Neal was deeply involved in every aspect of the case, and she felt empowered by a legal team that trusted her, included her, and respected her spirituality and her determination to right a perceived injustice. "The lawyers warned me about how nasty things would get," she says, "but because I really believed justice needed to be done, I was willing to go on. And they were with me all the way. It was almost as though they saw themselves as knights in shining armor, out to get justice not just for me, but also for the armed forces, who had been sold bad ammunition. They were principled warriors. When they destroyed a witness, it was only because they had so much evidence of lack of integrity. They never did it just to do it."

What Holloway and Leech found in Neal was a way of looking at life that had great power and energy behind it. In working with that energy, her lawyers realized they had a potent force on their side, an unshakable, determined, positive force. "We were really able to connect on the idea that there is something greater going on here, and that it means something," says Leech. At first, says Holloway, Neal seemed almost too good to be true. "It's funny, but when you have a client who is fundamentally honest, you tend at first to be skeptical. But then it was corroborated over and over again."

Conscious Litigation

Although Neal came to the case with a powerful desire to see justice done and a belief that everything happens for a reason, the experience took a toll on her. It was the way she responded to the setbacks, however, that kept her moving forward, often stronger for the pain.

She remembers entering her first deposition with her usual open-hearted attitude, "being loving to everyone involved and so on. But they attacked me viciously. They were horrible. They asked demeaning questions; they cut me off. I had the sense that Honeywell was trying to do everything possible to make me feel bad, so that I would discontinue the case." When she left the room five hours later, she felt dizzy and sick to her stomach. She could hardly walk. When the Honeywell lawyers announced that they would need a second deposition, Neal became determined not to have the same experience again. "I realized I had to be a spiritual warrior, to fight for what I needed to do and draw on resources I didn't know I had."

She enlisted a therapist with a spiritual background to prepare her for her next deposition. The woman told Neal that the lawsuit would help her heal from an incident that took place when she was seven, when her father became angry and chased and beat her. Her mother, in the other room, had not come to her aid.

The therapist also told Neal that, in this case, she should forget about having an open heart and being loving. "She said, 'Don't do that with people who are out to hurt you,'" she recalls. Instead, the woman recommended that Neal do a daily grounding meditation in which she was to picture herself as a tall tree sending roots down into the ground and taking nourishment from the earth. Then, during the deposition, she was to imagine herself being inside a luminous egg, and that any evil intent that came her way would bounce right off it. "She said, 'Remember that this is your time to fight for your truth. And you'll always have the lawyers there to protect you.'"

At the second deposition, Neal felt like a new person. "I was so calm and so strong that I was able to answer questions clearly," she says. "I didn't feel threatened or attacked. I pictured their verbal lunges just bouncing off me. It was quite amazing. Three hours into it, the lawyer who was questioning me started banging his head on his arms, which were crossed on the desk in front of him. He said, 'That's it; I've got nothing more to ask.' What a different experience it was. Although I was very scared about the trial, I knew from that experience that I had the strength to take it on."

At Trial

A month before the trial was set to start, Neal began doing her daily grounding meditation once again. She also changed her diet after a friend suggested that eating root vegetables might help her feel more grounded. "I know it sounds New Age-y," she says, "but every time I ate a carrot or a beet or anything else from the ground, it reminded me of my roots. So it became part of the practice." Realizing that the trial would probably last quite a while, she worked to build physical endurance by resuming the yoga practice she'd had off and on for years.

"It had to be a holistic preparation," she says. "It had to be spiritual, physical, and emotional. The lawyers had said that they'd fight for me but that I was the one who would win the case. I had to know the case better than they did. They had sent copies of all the documents to my home and told me my homework was to know the case inside out, to look for inconsistencies in their story, and always to remember what the truth was."

During the trial, her preparation paid off. "Because of my contemplative practices and the studying I had done, I was 100 percent aware of every word, every connection," she says. It empowered me and made me a full member of the team. I was one of them for that short period of time, which was a wonderful experience."

To Leech, the proof that Neal's preparation was valuable was evident in the quality of her presence. "There's this theological notion of living under God's grace. Paul talks about it in Galatians. The idea is that you're completely free. There's nothing to be embarrassed or ashamed of. You're accepted and are perfectly all right the way you are. There's tremendous peace in that. I really don't know how Judi gets to that understanding, but I saw that characteristic and quality in her." Both Leech and Holloway shake their heads in wonder as they reminisce about Neal's testimony and the fact that she enjoyed giving it so much. "She weathered it so well because she didn't have to worry much about what would come out," Leech says. "She had done such extensive and detailed preparation."

During that preparation, there arose what Leech says could have been a grueling moral dilemma—except that the client involved was Neal. "You often see clients in these difficult positions," he says. "The question is, Are you going to tell the truth or aren't you?" What happened was this: in the middle of the case, Neal called Leech and Holloway's attention to a document they hadn't seen before, a journal of hers—in fact a kind of dream log—from the time of the events in question. It corroborated what Neal had told them and spoke to her mental state at the time. "It was a document of tremendous relevance to the case, and it laid bare a number of personal and embarrassing facts," Leech says. Neal never hesitated. She gave the document to her lawyers straightaway.

"We wrestled with the question: Are we obligated to turn it over?" Leech recalls. "It was so intensely personal. With any other client, if they had a clue they might be obligated to turn it over, you wonder if you'd see it in the first place. Then, once having gotten it, you might have a struggle about turning it over to the other side. With Judi, it was a foregone conclusion that we'd do what we needed to do. And she's no dummy: she knew what it would mean for the other side to have it." Leech and Holloway even considered dropping a claim for emotional distress so that the judge would review the document and maybe not require that they hand it over. But for Neal, it was a simple matter of integrity.

She didn't hold back any personal information, even the parts that might hurt her case. "I told them all they needed to know," she says, "everything that could come up. And the things I warned them about became points of contention." For example, Honeywell claimed that Neal left her job in Joliet not because she was hounded out in retaliation for exposing a massive fraud on the government, but because she wanted to start a new life with her lover. When both her former husband and the person Honeywell said was her lover testified, they both gave the lie to Honeywell's version of events.

Now when she recalls her time on the witness stand, it is with something approaching glee. "I remember Honeywell trying to destroy me on the stand," she recalls. "It was almost laughable. I was up there five different times for a total of fifteen hours, and I was never impeached (this is confirmed in at least one order, written by the trial judge in response to posttrial motions by Honeywell). We impeached them once or twice per witness. It gave me such confidence that what I was doing was right. I was unshakable, strong. I did my spiritual practices to help keep me centered, my meditation and prayer. And the experience of being on the stand, which is normally so traumatic, was for me almost joyful because I knew so clearly what was true." That clarity had a profound effect on the jury. The foreman, in discussing the case with Leech and Holloway after the trial, said he and his fellow jurors had seen Neal as nothing less than a hero.

Leech says it is Neal's openness to experience that made her such a terrific witness. "She is not prone to protect herself as other people do," Leech says. "In every moment, she has a sense of the big picture. She is by finding a legal tactic to circumvent a difficult situation, he not only would have compromised Neal's integrity, but also would have undermined a process that depended on her honesty and faith in the truth for its power and potence.

Working with Neal taught Leech to be open to clients' wisdom—not always easy when you're caught up in the whipsaw rhythm of litigation. "If a person has found some sort of spiritual path, it's important to acknowledge that and respect it," he says. "You have to take it seriously and be open to the fact that there might be a wisdom in that person that goes beyond the worldly and may even be superior to it. Lawyers need to realize that clients in given situations may seem unwise, but if they go into those situations with their eyes open, maybe they're wiser than we are. At least we shouldn't be so sure our wisdom is superior."

Although Leech says he wouldn't hold Neal up as an example to just any client, for someone who is spiritual he wouldn't hesitate. "I'd talk about doing some spiritual work or some discipline to help them keep the long view in mind," he says. "Maybe meditation, or maybe I'd simply suggest immersing yourself in spiritual works or in a class or in Bible study—some form of being focused on things that detach you from your focus on the case—for two reasons: one, to get some degree of mental health during the process; and two, so that you'll perform more effectively in the case."

In representing Judi Neal, Leech may have peered into the future. A Cultural Creative if there ever was one, Neal embodies a combination of qualities that Leech finds exemplary—in a client and in a person. "I think she's a wonderful role model," he says. "There's a tendency among people with business backgrounds, people who are bottom-line oriented and successful in business or law, to be very worldly and to try to take control. They tend to look down on, or to not take seriously, people who come across as being more open and less hard-driving, and who acknowledge they have a spiritual life.

"Judi is a good role model for a businessperson because she has a tough-minded business sense. She can call the tough shots and stand up under attack. But at the same time, she is a very open, generous, and spiritual person. I don't mean to idealize her, but that, to me, makes her a great role model."

In pondering what it might mean to lawyers if more spiritually minded clients begin flowing into their offices, Leech mentions a pet

very centered." Leech understood that in Neal he had a spec
client, one whose dedication to spiritual values made the ent
more exciting and, in ways, deeper than usual for him. For th
of the case, the issues that concerned Neal and her legal tea
their very depths, to the kind of people they are, what they b
be right, and what their roles were in one another's lives.

Neal says she was able to bring so much of herself to bear o
and to sustain her focus only because it was a partnership—
and Leech were right there with her.

"I was in awe of the power and the radicalness of our lega
There I was, this one little person, taking on a huge corpora
these incredibly powerful people were put on the stand. They
choice of telling the truth or getting caught in their lies. The
face me and what they'd done to me, and I was able to get justi
Where else in the world could you do that?"

Looking Back

Because he too has an active spiritual life, Leech was able to
Neal in conversations that many lawyers would have avoided.
appreciated and welcomed her overtly spiritual take on experien(
most clients would have chosen not to express, even if they felt th
way. At one point, Neal asked Leech to accompany her into an ant
off the courtroom for a moment of silence and to recognize the pr
with them that day of a Hinshaw & Culbertson partner who was
case at the beginning but died shortly thereafter.

In the spiritual bond he established with Neal and, to a lesser d
with a few previous clients, Leech says he sees real practical valu
gives you a lot of tools you wouldn't otherwise have," he says. Sud
the technical legal fix is only one piece of a picture that has a broa(
context, one in which the language of reconciliation and the conc(
being made whole have new ramifications. Lawyers typically try to
clients cope with difficult realities—being fired, being sued, or o
wise having one's dignity affronted—but someone who believes tha
inner life is too important to keep hidden, even in the context of a
dispute, offers a lawyer sensitive to that position a new context f
which to come at the problem. "As a lawyer, you have to be sensitiv
what these people are going through," says Leech. He recalls the s
ation with the dream journal, noting that if he had tried to interv

theory of his—that lawyers tend to resemble their clients. This, he says, explains much of the public's current disdain for the legal profession: people see their own less-than-flattering qualities reflected in the legal profession. "After all, civility, respect, trust, and so on, are in pretty short supply in society generally," he says. This, he contends, has major implications for any trend in society. "If there is a spiritual movement—whether it is New Age or something more traditional—we as lawyers will have to resemble our clients; otherwise we won't have them anymore."

THE NEW CORPORATE CLIENT

For Carolyn Forehand, having the opportunity to resemble her client—she has just one—has been the best thing that ever happened to her career. The client is the Nashville-based physician-management company PhyCor, for which Forehand is vice president and general counsel. A $2 billion company, PhyCor started an industry when it began managing clinics in 1988. Spiritual values are of such importance to the company's leadership that in 1998 it scuttled plans to merge with another large company in the field because of concerns that their values might clash.

Much like Judi Neal, on the individual level, PhyCor is an example of a "new client," a type that is becoming increasingly common in the business world. Such concepts as values-based management and servant-leadership—which have been discussed among executives for some years now—are bearing fruit in organizations that understand the value of *values* in creating coherent and resilient corporate cultures. Several celebrated studies (most notably those by Collins and Porras) have shown that doing good is not only personally satisfying but also quite profitable.

Spiritual values inform every facet of PhyCor's culture. "The company was built around a do-the-right-thing mentality," says Forehand. "It's a simple phrase that is often used in very complex situations." One way that mentality is expressed is in an emphasis on building long-term relationships, which is reflected in relationships with outside vendors. "We use one law firm above all others while some companies bounce back and forth from law firm to law firm. But the important thing among the businesspeople here is nurturing that relationship."

As a lawyer, Forehand—who was previously a partner in a Nashville law firm—is most impressed and inspired by the PhyCor leadership's attitude about her and her staff's role. "The philosophy here is really deeply embedded in the structure of the company," she says. "Often I'll have the right contract in a given situation; it's on my side. But they say it's not right. They won't take advantage of having the contractual ability to do something to somebody. For example, our employment agreements contain strict noncompete clauses. Some people have left. As a lawyer, I could come up with legal arguments about how our restrictive covenants could prevent them from taking another job. But the employer says that in most cases it won't hurt the company at all if they do. They'll say, 'I don't care what the contract says; there's no reason to prevent a former employee from taking the job.'

"Many clients put the lawyer out front to be the bad guy. These people aren't like that. They put the relationships first and use their legal counsel to advise on what they decide as a business perspective. Nothing here is as adversarial as it was in private practice."

For Forehand, it's a tremendous relief to be supported for doing what feels right to her. The company's founder has shared his philosophy with her, explaining how important it is to live each day as though what you do might change the world. She recalls a time when, having worked a full day on a particularly mundane project, she was feeling rather low, and the founder paid her a visit. "He came over and told me to remember that I was doing work to provide for the growth of the company and to provide people with jobs," she recalls. "He showed me that there was a higher purpose to what I was doing than just making money and having nice things."

Working for such people, Forehand says, gives her a great sense of security. It has made practicing law a more rewarding experience than she had come to think possible because the company's emphasis on integrity, which consistently trumps the zeal to maximize profits, tells her that she is valued as a person with a unique contribution to make—not just as a technician. She has never had to wonder whether the company would be there for her in times of family crisis; they have. Nor is there any question that they might ask her to do things professionally that are not consistent with her values. "Here, you're not out to nail the other person, or to get bragging rights, or to request something that isn't fair. Some lawyers behave in ways that you tend to dismiss as just being how a lawyer's supposed to behave. That sort of behavior would never be tolerated by the principals for whom I work. I am never pressured to be anything other than a good person, and that really frees you to actually be a good person.

"I've told my husband that when you're at work every day and people say, 'I'm so glad you're here,' and 'Thank you for what you're doing,' and 'You're such a big help,' well, it's just wonderful. In private practice, all you'd ever hear was, 'When are you going to have that document?' 'When will you get this done?'"

LESSONS FOR THE BAR

Lawyers spend a good deal of time trying to read trends in business and society that might help them predict what the next hot practice area is likely to be. The examples at the beginning of this chapter, along with Neal's lawsuit, Carolyn Forehand's experience at PhyCor, and Ray's findings on "Cultural Creatives," suggest that substantive practice areas are only part of the story. The other part has to do with attitude and orientation. A lawyer who is sensitive to clients' spiritual leanings—one who can understand and acknowledge their potential role in the process—may be able to facilitate solutions that a more traditional practitioner would never even consider, solutions that speak to the client's need for integrity and meaning.

Lawyers with a holistic bent see it as part of their job to help clients make sense—intellectual, emotional, and spiritual—of the predicaments that bring them to seek a lawyer's help. If current trends are any indication, more and more clients will probably be open to—may even seek—this kind of counsel. For them, having a lawyer who is attuned to inner-life issues will be at least as important as having one who has common sense and technical ability.

It's important to remember that stepping into the legal arena can be a bewildering experience, one that often makes people lose their balance and doubt their own perceptions. Both Judi Neal and her lawyer, Michael Leech, make it clear that there are practices and techniques that can help clients feel clearer and stronger as they enter unfamiliar territory. For lawyers who make it their business to understand their clients' trepidations and can then offer suggestions on how they can prepare and strengthen themselves for the road ahead, the rewards, in terms of both personal satisfaction and client loyalty, will be plentiful.

Transforming Your Practice

It's always best, when a new client comes calling, to suspend judgment about who he or she is. The truth is, you really don't know. What matters to one client may be utterly irrelevant to another, and the source of a client's values or goals may elude or, perhaps, surprise you. Try to keep in mind that clients are changing; they're becoming more willing to lead their lives in ways that reflect their moral and spiritual values. If you feel that way, too, perhaps you can see your professional collaborations as opportunities to deepen yourself through your work. And keep a few things in mind:

- When you take on a new client, it's hard to tell at first where the energy is going to come from, how your approaches to the problem will blend to fuel your collaboration. Don't rule out possible sources of strength or wisdom simply because they don't fall into the usual boxes.
- If you feel like exploring new ways to work with and relate to your clients—perhaps using a more integrative approach—try not to simply assume that they aren't open to alternatives. Check it out—tactfully.
- Spend some time trying to understand what values and beliefs clients bring with them to your office. You may find that, with their input, you can craft creative solutions that are custom-tailored not only to their particular legal needs, but also to their temperaments and convictions. And you may very well earn their undying respect and gratitude in the process.
- If you're looking for a job, consider taking an in-house position at a company with a reputation for putting relationships above profits and people's needs above expedience.

CHAPTER TWELVE

LEGAL EDUCATION
AT THE THRESHOLD

Work enables us to put our personal stamp
of approval, our own watermark, the autograph
of our souls on the development of the world.
In fact, to do less is to do nothing at all.

—*Joan Chittister*

CLEARY, CRACKS ARE SHOWING in the legal facade.

Leading lawyers and law professors are beginning to speak out against rampant adversarialism, pointing out that the combative approach may have its place in the culture but that it has simply spread too far. Overwhelmingly, their words are falling on supportive ears. At the same time, groups such as the International Alliance of Holistic Lawyers and others who are exploring the merits of such concepts as restorative—rather than retributive—justice and "therapeutic jurisprudence" are espousing and practicing an approach to law that sees the client as a whole person with emotional and spiritual needs, someone who is embedded in the complex web of familial and community relationships.

More impetus for change is coming from clients like Judi Neal, who look to the legal system to solve their problems in ways that address their needs as multidimensional people. Law schools are changing, too, as they gradually begin adding programs and courses that seek to reverse a long-standing tendency to see students' previous lives as largely irrelevant to the process of creating lawyers.

A Course Correction: Northeastern University

David Hall is one voice for change. The former dean of Northeastern University's School of Law, he worries about an educational experience that asks students to leave behind their deepest values and beliefs as the price of earning a law degree. He believes it is time for lawyers to reclaim the "higher ground" of soul and spirit—abandoned, he says, to "mystics and skeptics"—and help others discover it for the first time. "The cure to what ails us as a profession is in this area, lying dormant inside so many of the people we train and so many of the lawyers engaged in practice," he says.

Hall notes that because lawyers are so much more comfortable with "doing" than they are with "being," they have defined the entire profession in a way that reflects this predilection. *Activities*, such as writing briefs, making oral arguments, and, ultimately, winning cases, are too often seen as the whole point of the legal enterprise. Indeed, these are the skills that academicians are comfortable asking students to hone; only rarely do they cross over into less hard-edged concerns. To Hall, the primary casualties of this focus on doing are students' values, their sense of self—and their ability to connect, empathize, love, and care for other people. "To have a healthy profession, we have to spend time developing both parts of ourselves, because they go together," he says.

In 1997, Hall, along with John Hamilton, managing partner of Boston's 360-lawyer Hale and Dorr, began a collaboration designed to answer a question that they found especially compelling: How can we start a conversation about what it means to be a lawyer that gets to the very heart of what we, as human beings, are here to do as practitioners?

At sixty-five, Hamilton, a pillar of the local legal community, understands as well as anyone the obstacles that prevent lawyers from finding satisfaction in their work. Prior to the collaboration with Northeastern, he served on a Boston Bar Association committee on professional fulfillment, making him keenly aware of the levels of burnout, depression, and general unhappiness among his colleagues. He came to the law in a different era, grew to love the practice, and now spends a fair amount of time pondering what can be done to prepare people coming into the law, on the emotional and spiritual levels, so that they will be able to find the kind of pleasure in legal work that he has long enjoyed.

To find out what lay beyond work as usual, Hall and Hamilton oversaw the creation of an innovative course on professional development at Northeastern with an emphasis on personal fulfillment and leadership. It involved twenty students, two professors (including Hall), and three Hale and Dorr partners (one was Hamilton himself).

In initial discussions, Hall and the other Northeastern professors, along with their Hale and Dorr counterparts, determined that it usually takes a dramatic event such as divorce or a serious illness to make lawyers who feel lost, unhealthy, and out of touch with themselves sit up and really look at where they are in their lives. The question vis-à-vis the new course then became clear: How do you get people into a setting where they will undergo that kind of reassessment without the provocation of such a crisis? The answer lay in a unique combination of weekly classroom sessions and extensive readings on such issues as family and balance, the future of the profession, creativity, and change—all bracketed by two retreats, an initial weekend in the country west of Boston and a final one-day session at the same site. The retreats involved not only physical challenges such as walking across ropes and wires suspended fifty feet in the air and secured by colleagues on the ground— designed to build trust among participants—but also open discussions, quiet time for reflection, and group readings.

From the beginning, it was made clear that, for the purposes of the retreat, titles and hierarchies would be irrelevant. Everyone was to participate at the same level, in situations that made it difficult, if not impossible, to hide. The course's stress on deep reflection was played out both in the process of journal writing and in bringing the fruit of that inner work into the outer world, through frank discussions about life and work and how the two can become one.

Another emphasis was on taking risks, going beyond self-imposed physical and emotional comfort zones to get out of the box of daily life. Many participants say that by challenging themselves to be open and real in a supportive, nurturing environment, they were able to feel "seen," by others and by themselves, in a way they hadn't been before. Deep professional issues came to the fore—Is my work really an expression of who I am? What kind of a contribution can I make through the law? Are my "work self" and my "family self" the same self?—and there was the sense of an entire group's being engaged in the crucial work of taking its bearings, individually and as a whole.

The course changed lives. Participants gained a sense that real fulfillment in law comes not only from mastering the law itself, but also from establishing deep connections with colleagues and clients. Others decided that it is essential to find ways to balance the "doing" life of the lawyer with the "being" experiences that all people need in order to maintain their vitality.

The Hale and Dorr partners came to realize that there is a risk that the hothouse environment of big-firm law will cut lawyers off from life outside, and that it is crucial for them to take time to reconnect with the sense of purpose that brought them to the practice in the first place. Hamilton now has a special managing partner's bookshelf in the firm's library where he offers texts that speak to quality-of-life issues as well as to more overtly spiritual themes. He oversees an active program of seminars and longer courses for the firm on stress reduction and contemplative practices, and has instituted a regular retreat for new associates. Nowadays, when Hale and Dorr hires new lawyers, Hamilton emphasizes that one reason they were hired is for their values. "Don't check them at the door," he tells them.

For students in the program, studies of substantive law suddenly took on a human dimension that had previously been missing for them. They also gained a unique way to assess their course in the future. The seminar required that they write letters to themselves, laying out their beliefs and feelings about life and law. They then turned them over to the dean, whose office will send them back to the students in two or three years. That way, they'll have at least one occasion on which to evaluate how well they've held to a vision they articulated at a quieter, more reflective time.

Second-year law student Toly Siamos enrolled in the Northeastern/ Hale and Dorr professional development program to meet the Hale and Dorr partners and perhaps enhance his chances of getting a job at the firm. How ironic then that—after really connecting with fellow students whom he had always kept at arm's length, talking to the partners of a prestigious law firm on a level he had never thought possible, discovering the mind- and emotion-expanding possibilities of writing in a journal, and "crying more than once"—he finished the program convinced that his path, at least in the near future, had nothing whatever to do with large-firm practice.

Siamos, who is twenty-four, grew up being told that he would make a great lawyer. But what really interested him was law enforcement, and before entering law school he spent some time as a reserve police officer in his native Falmouth, Massachusetts. But he knew he would never get rich fighting crime, and his parents, Greek immigrants, always stressed how important it was to be "a success."

Siamos entered law school thinking the law would be his ticket to success as his parents, and he too, understood the word. But after the course, he declined a job offer from a large firm. Instead, he took an unpaid internship in the state attorney general's office, where he had a chance to sharpen his oral advocacy skills, something he'd always wanted to do.

The Northeastern/Hale and Dorr course helped him realize that it was OK to let go of pursuing a corporate career. Siamos's plan now is to look for a job at a law enforcement agency such as the FBI. "The thing is, if I was to, say, work thirty kidnapping cases and even if I was successful in solving just one, I think I'd feel truly fulfilled," he says. "On the other hand, if I help corporation A sue corporation B, or help the shareholders of A sue corporation B, I'll make a lot of money, and it will bring me things I like, but at the end of the day I'll be alone. I won't have any time to develop relationships or to do the other things that are important in life.

"The course helped me not be afraid to step out and say I want to try this for a while. And it gave me a sense of ease about trying several things in my career and trying to fulfill myself in as many ways as I can."

Lawyers are hungry for connection, to their own inner lives and to each other, and coming together in a way that allows them to experience those connections is both incredibly powerful and, ultimately, healing. The Northeastern course, which David Hall calls the most exciting educational experience of his life, helped participants recall their value as human beings—beyond the number of hours they bill or their class standing. The program, now a regular part of Northeastern's curriculum, has attracted a good deal of attention from both law schools and law firms that realize lawyers, the legal profession, and the public all deserve better than what they've now got, and that something bold and new is needed if a true transformation is to occur.

Cultivating Compassion: Suffolk University

Another experiment in bringing a deeper awareness to the study of law takes place every semester at Suffolk University School of Law, amid a row of eighteenth-century brownstones a block behind the Massachusetts State House in Boston. There, Cheryl Conner, a Harvard-trained former federal prosecutor, offers a course called "The Reflective Lawyer: Peace Training for Lawyers."

The course is offered as a companion seminar for students in Suffolk's clinical program, a place to go with the thoughts and feelings that arise in the course of their work at, say, children's legal services, the U.S. Attorney's Office, or the state legislature.

Students tend to enroll in the class because they feel disenfranchised from the narrow focus of legal education on doctrine. The course gives them a place to talk about values and express their fears. Common among them: that the practice of law will crush their souls, cause them to betray themselves, or make them feel burned-out and angry.

"They're delighted to have a place to talk about their values in law school," Conner says. She provides them with that, and with something more—a secular presentation of the Buddhist approach to conflict resolution. She also gives them tools such as meditation and visualization to relieve stress and focus awareness. And she asks them to look into their own pasts, at whatever "wisdom traditions" they may have grown up with, for ways to conceptualize—and then behave in—challenging situations.

Conner is troubled by the glorified model of the detached, analytical, warrior-like lawyer, feeling that such glorification can undermine appreciation of the lawyer's role as a wise problem-solver and healer. "We may even have squelched the evolution of top-rate, skillful lawyers who are not afraid to expose their hearts," she says. To counteract that model, she espouses the integration of lessons from lawyers' own traditions with their daily law practices and feels that, in most cases, they can enrich their practices, rather than finding it necessary to change careers or specialties.

The class is something of a cutting-edge laboratory, a place where students are offered tools to integrate heart and mind with the hope that, by doing so at this stage of their legal careers, they will have a chance to go into practice as whole people and perhaps even stay that way. The key here is that they are not cultivating these skills in a vacuum. They are using them in actual clinical settings, giving them a chance to hold spiritual theory and practice up against actual experience in the legal trenches.

For some students, the class has been a career saver, having convinced them—after a fair bit of soul-searching—that the law really is the profession for them. Their substantive classes give them the technical knowledge a legal career requires; Conner's class provides a way to cultivate their inner wisdom, so that they can use that knowledge both compassionately and responsibly.

Second-year student Nadia Ballis speaks for many of Conner's students: "At one point, I wanted to drop out of law school. But Cheryl's class made me want to stay. It was so encouraging, especially to find out that other people felt the same way. I had met a lot of lawyers, and a lot of them were frustrated and quite stressed out. I realized that other people are struggling with the same issues, and it became clear to me that it is possible to remain humanistic, to have a heart, while being a lawyer. I realized that you have to work at it, but you really have more choice than you might think to bring your values into the practice."

Conner's approach to understanding what law practice demands of lawyers and what lawyers have the right to ask of the practice has vastly expanded her students' concept of the terrain they will encounter after school. They have been given ways to think about the practice that can accommodate who they are not only as processors of legal information but also as human beings. In Conner's class, compassion, empathy, and the easing of others' suffering are not tangential to the legal endeavor. They are central, the primary sources of satisfaction and even joy.

"I was a very spiritual person in college—not religious, but spiritual. But I've found that in law school, there's no place for that," says Darren Rubin, a third-year student. "The message is you'd better seal it away while you're here and stick to linear thinking. But in Cheryl's class, I had an opportunity to explore other parts of being human, rather than just drafting contracts or analyzing cases. Here, I found a spiritual outlet."

In 1997, Conner became the first law professor ever to receive a Contemplative Practice Fellowship from the Nathan Cummings Foundation.

The fellowships, administered by the American Council of Learned Societies, are given to scholars to further their research in contemplation-related activities. The goal is to create a new curriculum focused on contemplative practice. "The Reflective Lawyer" is Conner's attempt to move in that direction.

Charles Halpern, a lawyer and former law school dean who heads the Nathan Cummings Foundation, says he was surprised to see a law

---

 The Compassionate Prosecutor

Boston native Tom Kaplanes came to Conner's class with a moral, ethical, and spiritual tradition that meant a great deal to him. Greek Orthodox by faith, and a person with strong family ties, he came hoping to answer a simple question: Is it possible to maintain the values of his heritage and still pursue his goal of becoming a prosecutor?

He answered the question after reflecting on a case from his clinical work at the U.S. Attorney's Office in which a former Boston police sergeant was convicted for smuggling heroin into the country. "We had been talking in class about the Four Thoughts of Buddhism [in addition to the Four Immeasurables, see p. 168], which include forgiveness," he says. "Then, as I sat next to the prosecutor in the courtroom during the sentencing, I remember thinking, 'This is probably one of the most heinous crimes imaginable. This guy was entrusted to uphold the law and protect citizens from such crimes, yet he has turned around and betrayed the citizens of this city.'"

In class, Kaplanes commented on how hard it was to feel any compassion for the former sergeant, either as a defendant or as a person. But after discussing what it really means to have compassion, he came to see that it didn't mean wanting him to get a shorter sentence, "or just turning the other cheek because Christ might have done that." What he learned is that it is possible to forgive someone but not forgive what the person did, keeping in mind that forgiveness does not necessarily mean demanding less severe punishment.

The realization had important implications for his future career. He finds it satisfying to know that the prosecutor's job is to dispense justice but that he need not go through the work being "ironfisted" and ignoring his heart. Ultimately, he says of the class, "We learned that we will not be seen as three-headed circus animals if we act in a humane way as lawyers."

professor applying for a fellowship. Although the Foundation was keenly interested in getting people from diverse disciplines into the program, it hadn't occurred to him that law might be one of those disciplines. But after reflecting, Halpern says, he realized it made perfect sense for someone to bring contemplative practice into law school. "It's small wonder," he says, "that when Cheryl offers a course at Suffolk that promises that students will be able to bring with them the totality of who they are, there would be an enormous response."

INTEGRATING PROFESSIONAL AND SPIRITUAL VALUES

It was a spiritual search that led Conner herself to Suffolk in 1995. After law school, she practiced for fifteen years—first in the statehouse as an assistant attorney general, then as counsel to the Massachusetts Senate, and finally as an assistant U.S. Attorney—before moving on to Suffolk. In the meantime, she became a practicing Buddhist.

As a U.S. Attorney, she tried hard to be compassionate, to be sensitive to the suffering she saw around her while seeing the bigger picture that it was all part of. Each day, she tried to bring as little aggression, extra verbiage, or gossip as possible to her work. But it was lonely. She sought—but never found—a community of peers with whom to reflect on how best to bring their own wisdom, not just their legal prowess, to their work.

Because Conner never did find such a group with which to share her thoughts and feelings about the inner work of trying cases, it ultimately proved too hard to reconcile courtroom combat with her spiritual path. Since turning from law practice to teaching, however, she has started to speak out about her conviction that even litigation—when handled with compassion, integrity, and skill—is thoroughly compatible with spirituality.

In "The Reflective Lawyer," Conner offers students permission to integrate spiritual and professional values. Many, she notes, have already received messages about the dualistic split—between themselves and clients, themselves and the other side, between their minds and their hearts. "There has been an active discouragement of people bringing their hearts to the profession," she says. "We demean it; it's always been seen as the concern of social workers."

"The Reflective Lawyer" helps each student find his or her own way to heal that split. One practice Conner uses in her class and finds

particularly effective is analytical meditation. It is unusual, she
that it acknowledges that the mind has two distinct qualities—aι
getic, discursive quality; and a restful, spacious quality. Lawyers
to have a hard time sitting still and quieting their minds but are vε
good at using their intellects to take a concept and explore it. Analytica.
meditation suits them well because it uses this strength in the service of
exploring concepts that are beneficial to everyone, such as Buddhism's
Four Immeasurables—compassion, equanimity, joy, and love. A brief
meditation exercise on compassion might be conducted as follows:

Step 1: Sit quietly and think back to a recent case that tugged
at your heartstrings. (Example: Perhaps a client's lack of
intellectual or emotional resources led her to put herself in
a compromising and painful position.)

Step 2: Try to really feel your way into that client's shoes.

Step 3: Then, think beyond that particular client to other people
who are likely to have suffered in a similar way.

Step 4: Cultivate a heartfelt wish that all those people would be
free from suffering.

The point of this exercise is simple but profound: it undercuts the
mind's predilection to avoid thinking of such things—much the way
most people look away from beggars on the street. "This way," says Conner, "you affirmatively bring the mind back to suffering, and you say,
'Wow, it's here; I wish the best for that person.' You are training your
mind not to avert from, but to take on, the suffering and wish it would
go away."

Conner points out that for thousands of years, this kind of
thinking—which is evident in many traditions, including Christian
prayer—has helped people get beyond themselves and find compassion for family, friends, community, and strangers. It offers a way of
opening your heart and giving yourself practice in keeping it open.
The idea is to use the mind's natural tendency to be busy—to chew on
things endlessly—to get out of the loop of typical workaday content
now and then, and instead ponder something that gives life more texture and depth.

After a meditation that, like the preceding, emphasizes the mind's
discursive quality, Conner asks students to honor the mind's capacity for

"openness and spaciousness," by doing a simple "calm abiding" meditation. "I ask them to simply sit and bring their awareness into their bodies and their breath and the room around them, and simply practice being and breathing." An example can be found on the facing page.

Another concept that can be quite beneficial for lawyers is that of impermanence, which Conner teaches by asking students to think about all the relationships in their lives that came and went—family members who have died, cousins who moved, romantic relationships that ended. "Say you're in an intense meeting," she explains. "You can't imagine anything but the importance of getting the right result. It feels like the most real, solid thing in the world. But if you could suddenly think about impermanence, you would realize that your client is going to die, that you'll go on to have a zillion more feelings, moments, concerns; that your career is unlikely to live or die based on how you handle this one case."

STAYING TRUE TO YOURSELF

Conner came of age in the 1960s, enamored with the idea of using the law to help the community. Now she's interested in something different: how lawyers can transform themselves in order to be more compassionate, wise, and effective in every walk of lawyering. "How can you be the most effective corporate transactional lawyer, for example?" she asks.

One solution is to revive the use of language that evokes our wisdom traditions. "We all have those traditions, but we're discouraged from

---

 Calm Abiding Meditation Exercise

This exercise will help to relax, refresh, and refocus your mind.

Step 1: Sit comfortably with your back straight, feet resting on the floor and hands in your lap.

Step 2: Bring your awareness to your body. Where does it feel relaxed? Where is it tense?

Step 3: Breathe deeply to a count of four and exhale to a count of eight.

Step 4: Simply practice being and breathing.

using the language that evokes them. We generally don't hear about friendship with clients or having love and respect for attorneys in our community. You lose a lot when you don't use that language."

In the suffering Conner sees both in law practice and in the larger world, she says that, for lawyers, there is endless opportunity for compassion, healing, and spiritual growth. Satisfaction is there to be had, but it takes diligence and a deep desire to cultivate it and to grow. Conner, like David Hall of Northeastern University, insists that lawyers must learn to *be* as well as to do, must muster the courage to care and let it show, and must realize that only by building a path that expresses who they truly are will they find the deepest kind of satisfaction in their work and leave the profession better than they find it.

Mapping New Terrain

Both the Northeastern/Hale and Dorr program and Cheryl Conner's innovative class at Suffolk are helping to expand the traditional law school map. Conner's student Tom Kaplanes says he's become aware of brand-new pathways: "Instead of going down route 1, you realize you can go down the back roads and see what you've been missing." For the seasoned pros involved in the Northeastern program, that lesson was equally compelling, and all have vowed to take their bearings at regular intervals to make sure that the path they're on is still taking them where they truly want to go.

Although the Northeastern and Suffolk ventures are at the cutting edge in emphasizing personal growth and spirituality in legal academia, other schools are beginning to move in a similar direction, all of them looking to flesh out and integrate certain notions that have for too long been neglected, such as:

- Real fulfillment in law comes not only from mastering the law itself but also from establishing deep connections with colleagues and clients.
- It is essential to find ways to balance the "doing" life of the lawyer with the "being" experiences that all people need; vitality, creativity, and satisfaction require this balance.
- Great satisfaction comes from breaking out of the box of business-as-usual, making new connections, and tapping into sources of

creativity and love that ultimately must underlie real fulfillment in any profession.

- Regular reflection is essential, and without it, it is not possible to stay on course.
- Being true to yourself as a human being will make you a better, more satisfied lawyer.

 Yale Law School Retreat

In the fall of 1998, Yale Law School became the first in the nation to offer its students an opportunity to take an intensive meditation course. Twenty-two first-, second-, and third-year students spent four days sitting in silence, practicing yoga, and discussing themes of particular relevance to lawyers-to-be.

By all accounts, they had little trouble seeing the connection to the study and practice of law. According to Emily Bazelon, a Yale student who wrote about the retreat for the *Washington Post*, she and her classmates found a new context in which to understand what it means to be a lawyer, as well as a new use for their overachiever's intensity: making the switch from left brain to right.

One student said he planned to "root [his] feet to the ground" and listen to his breathing when, the following week, he argued his first opening motion in a courtroom.

In the contemplative environment of the retreat, the students, along with Yale faculty members and visiting lawyer-mediators, discussed various pertinent topics, including the role of contemplative practice in developing new strategies for listening to clients, and how the common tendency to make winning the highest goal can affect lawyers' thinking and quality of life.

In a session on what students hope to do before they die, the dreams they expressed showed great consistency: to really love someone, have children, leave a positive legacy, become a vehicle for achieving some public good, visit places that call to them. Not one person mentioned making a lot of money.

Mirabai Bush, director of the Center for Contemplative Mind in Society, which organized the retreat, said the students finished the program with enormous enthusiasm for continuing the practice. She added, "The whole experience made me feel better about the future than I had before."

For practicing lawyers, the emergence of such an awareness in law schools should come as good news for the future of the profession. New ideas about the relationship between "life" and work, along with an increasingly clear notion of what it means to be a *whole* lawyer, are just beginning to flow from law schools into the professional ranks. As the current gets stronger and the influence of younger lawyers increases, the support required to make a significant course correction will only grow.

CHAPTER THIRTEEN

THE CHOICE IS YOURS

One thing I've learned is that of all the horrendous problems
we face in the world, one strikes me as the root cause of them
all, and it's a myth: "I don't have any power."
—*Mark Dubois*
Director, Worldwise

Many people who have near-death experiences say that the
purpose of life is to grow in wisdom and learn how to love
better. You can do this as a doctor or not do it as a doctor.
You can do it as a street cleaner or not do it as a street cleaner.
It is not what you are doing, but whether or not you are
doing it with an open heart. That's what makes the difference.
—*Rachel Naomi Remen, M.D.*
Founder and director, Institute for the Study of Health and Illness

LAWYERS GET PAID GOOD MONEY for making the right choices. From a menu of options for accomplishing a given goal, they zero in on the best one, the one that will lead to a marginally—sometimes an infinitesimally—better result than the others. And yet, when it comes to their careers, they tend to have blind spots where choice is concerned. They can choose to leave one firm and go to work for another, or to expand their bankruptcy practice and scale back their M-and-A work without much trouble. But talk to them about choosing *how* they practice, how they can embody who they are in their work as lawyers, and they tend to glaze over or simply stare back uncomprehendingly.

It's the fashion these days to throw up your hands and run from such choices. The profession—and our world, for that matter—seems so unmoored, and so fraught with change, that it looks much easier to batten down the hatches, work as hard as you can, and let circumstance seal off your choices. After all, how much leeway do you really have, even in your own life?

Choosing to Choose

Until recently, Bruce Wagman was a happy associate at a twenty-five-lawyer San Francisco firm, where he had practiced employment litigation and insurance law since 1993. Then something happened. He was asked to make a decision that, for 99.9 percent of associates, would have been the easiest of their lives. But Wagman, always a .01 percent kind of guy, found the choice to be fiendishly difficult: he didn't know whether he wanted to accept an offer of partnership.

At first, he made it known that he would refuse outright, even though there was nowhere he would rather work. He loved his practice, and the firm had always been more than generous in funding the pro bono cases he was passionate about taking.

The problem was elsewhere. Even though partners assured him that little would change if he accepted their offer, there was a sticking point. It was the meeting. Once a month, on a Thursday night, the firm held a partnership meeting. "Even that to me was too much," Wagman recalls. "Just thinking of missing one night a month on Stinson Beach is hard, and twelve a year seemed like it might be enough to make me choose not to do it."

Wagman loves his home on the beach north of San Francisco with an unusual intensity. The partners knew this, and they promised him he wouldn't have to travel if he joined their ranks. That was crucial, because his daily four A.M. runs along the Pacific with his three dogs are sacred to him. He arrives at work in the city by six and he works hard and long. But he returns every night—right after work—to the beach house he shares with his wife.

It may seem odd, if not willfully perverse, that any lawyer would allow a twelve-night-a-year commitment to tip the scales against becoming a partner—particularly in a world where partnership is no longer the given it once was. But there is another way to look at it.

Wagman came to the law later than most, after working as an operating-room nurse for six years. He brought to the practice a clearer sense of who he is and what he wants from life—and from the law—than all but the rarest of younger lawyers. Anyone who knows him will attest to his clarity about what makes him happy. He knows, and jealously guards, the sources of his vitality—which have everything to do with sand and sea, and the special sense of place he feels at home. He refuses to cut himself off from that, or to cede his right to choose what works for him as a human being and as a lawyer. Too many lawyers, somehow unaware that they have a choice, make such sacrifices. Many end up feeling helpless and demoralized.

In the end, after putting off his decision as long as he could, Wagman decided to take the offer. He doesn't enjoy the meetings much, but he likes having more say about the kind of work he handles, and he particularly enjoyed being able to write down an outstanding bill for a client who is now nearly destitute.

Still, he continues to hold out his options. "I told them I'd try it," he says. "But I made it clear that if I don't like it, I'll go back to doing what I did before."

Whose Life Is It Anyway?

Arnold Kanter, a former large-firm partner who has consulted with Chicago law firms for the last seventeen years, is only too familiar with the sense of futility so many lawyers experience. "They seem to feel such a lack of control to do anything about the things that are bothering them," says Kanter. "It's as if it has all been imposed by outside forces, and there is nothing they can do."

There happens to be a lot they can do, according to Peter Cicchino, founder and head of the Lesbian and Gay Youth Project of the Urban Justice Center in New York City—if only they were clearer about what is at stake. "Our lives are the only things that are completely ours,"

Cicchino says. "The kind of life we make is the most important work, the single most important project we will ever undertake. One of the things that make me saddest when I talk to law students and lawyers is the recurring impression I get that they have lost a sense of their own agency, the sense that their lives are theirs to make of what they will. So people who are among the most gifted and privileged in the world instead live with a sense of drastically constricted possibilities of what they can do with their lives."

Cicchino speaks from experience. After a crisis of conscience caused him to leave the Jesuit order in the late 1980s, he decided that law school held out an opportunity to continue doing the kind of social justice work on which he thrives—the work he feels is the truest expression of who he is. Since graduating from Harvard Law School in 1992, he continues to do that work, in addition to teaching at American University Law School.

At some level, what disaffected lawyers appear to be saying is that the law has grown deaf to their needs. Thus, they feel helpless. They want to work in an environment that offers an opportunity to awaken to deeper levels of who they are, one that provides a way to express what matters most to them, allows them to make the contributions that only they can make, and provides a comfortable standard of living. They want their work to be part of their search for—and ultimately an expression of—what they feel to be an authentic life.

But how will that come about? Certainly not by waiting for some ill-defined perfect moment when the institutional problems that plague the profession suddenly vanish and a paradisiacal Eden replaces them. Even those most troubled by what the practice of law has become retain an inner awareness of its potential greatness. But to get there, lawyers must meet the status quo halfway, bringing their own transformative powers to bear, so that what is potentially sacred in the profession—those qualities that make people feel a calling to the law—becomes its *raison d'être*, and the headlong rush to ever increasing levels of wealth and power that has so gummed up the works begins to recede.

Regardless of profession, everyone has plenty to wake up to, greater depths to plumb. We live in a vortex of sights and sounds, demands and obligations, beauty and dross. If you don't take active measures to find out what really matters, no one will do it for you. Unless you control where you put your attention and your devotion, you will succumb to the usual distractions.

And it will become easy to make excuses, beginning with some version of the ever-popular "The client made me do it." In *The Soul of the Law*, psychologist-lawyer Benjamin Sells remarks on how, even though lawyers can be tough and articulate advocates for other people's positions, they often behave like children when it comes to standing up to what they perceive as their clients' unreasonable demands:

> I don't believe clients want lawyers to work too hard or act brutishly. And if they do? Well, then they must be reminded that they will get better representation from lawyers who are enjoying more of life's fullness than work alone can provide. . . . Adults . . . don't have to work themselves to death in their own profession. We don't have to retain outmoded systems that favor litigation over peacemaking. And adults don't have to treat other people shabbily just because somebody else tells us to.

For lawyers who work at cultivating awareness, the options that every moment presents to make a satisfying choice will become clearer all the time. It may mean discovering a new practice area or setting, one better suited to your particular emotional and, yes, spiritual needs. Occasionally—probably less often than you might think—it may mean leaving the profession. But often people come to see that they can blossom right where they're standing, finding deeper meaning in the material at hand or discovering other sources of sustenance that are more readily available than was at first apparent. If you have a spiritual bent, those possibilities are nearly endless.

Among the many ways you can exercise your own sense of agency within a law practice, and make the work an expression of who you are, are the following five options.

Choose Clients Carefully

One of the first choices you can make is one you often don't realize—or, in some cases, care to admit—is yours to make: whether or not to represent whoever walks through the door. Only you can decide when "No!" is the appropriate response when a would-be client comes knocking, but it's essential to realize the choice is yours to make.

After many years as a personal injury lawyer, Sheldon Tashman, profiled in Chapter 2, will not take a case he doesn't believe in. "My feeling is that everything you do because, for some reason, you think you're supposed to, is a chip off your self-image. The more whole your self-image is, the easier it is to make money the right way. It's so easy to take small cases, like soft-tissue cases, and build them up to make them look more serious than they are. I won't do that."

In a culture that labels him an "ambulance chaser," he has had to find his own standard of success, and he is no longer troubled when he meets people who suggest that his work is less than honorable. He knows differently. "I don't subscribe to the pervasive judgment that what I do isn't right, that it is somehow unclean," he says. "I take injury cases. And I help people. I know that what I do is looked down on, but I also know that I just got a guy money to help him cope with his paraplegia. I feel good about that. I'm satisfied with the work I do. And the truth is, there are shoddy people in every field.

"The law has many temptations that lack integrity," Tashman says. "There's the temptation to make a case out of nothing, to make a living out of situations that aren't real, to not be ethical. It's hard for me to live with doing things that don't feel right. In the past, when I did—and I'm not saying I broke any rules, just that certain things weren't really right—I had trouble sleeping. I'd think about someone catching me, and my son seeing me in the newspaper. It wasn't good to live with. Everything you do that's not kosher, every shortcut, makes things easier. But if you choose to live with integrity and not be uncomfortable with what you do, you have to care more, be more diligent, refuse cases that don't bear bringing, even though the culture says you'd be stupid not to—after all, money is money."

Stephen Chakwin, a New York City litigator who met Tashman when they opposed one another in a personal injury case, was inspired by his former opponent's example to make a significant transformation in his own practice. Early in 1998, Chakwin gave up his partnership at a medium-size New York law firm to go out on his own. He now works in a two-lawyer practice in New York and spends some time coaching unhappy lawyers toward finding a more satisfying path.

"What Shelly did was show me that even after a time in a very arid practice of law, it's possible to continue to be a human being, treat others as human beings, and still take good care of your clients," Chakwin says. "Now my fourteen-year-old daughter would say, 'Duh, Dad,' to that, but when for years you've been where everything is mind over matter—I don't mind, and you don't matter—it's easy to lose sight of that. In that environment, everyone seems to think that it's OK; they take it for granted, so you start to wonder if it's just you. In hindsight I see that it wasn't just me, and it's not that I am temperamentally unsuited to practice law, as I had begun to think maybe I was.

"Shelly showed me that the cost of practicing law was not as high as I thought it was. It doesn't have to be the dehumanizing chase for money or ego gratification that so many practitioners on both sides of the personal injury bar had turned it into," Chakwin says.

Try Treating People Differently

Once the decision to represent a client has been made, remaining mindful of the spiritual opportunities as the relationship unfolds can lead to real fulfillment—on the creative, ethical/moral, and human levels. Consider just a few of the junctures at which opportunities exist to enhance the interaction for you and for your client.

Even the partial list that follows is quite long. But it gets the point across: your choices are limited only by your imagination. Look at your interactions and see where you can open them up, illuminate motivation, seek direction, or find common ground.

Certain questions may bring key issues to the fore:

At the Initial Meeting:
Why has the client come? Is he driven by
  • anger?
  • a sense of having been victimized?
  • a desire to heal?
What does he expect of me?
What role does he want me to take?
What are my first impressions?
Am I listening as though he is the only other person on earth at the moment?
Have I turned off the phone or made arrangements for someone else to answer?
Am I seeing the whole person, or focusing narrowly on the possible legal issues?
Am I saying what I need to say to the client, or am I avoiding something?
Are my words consistent with my values?

Have I made clear what I see both his and my own role(s) to be in this relationship?

Have I made clear where my loyalties lie—to him, yes, but perhaps also to minimizing conflict, to the other side, or to the community?

Have I been clear about the range of options, both legal and non-legal, that may be available?

Have I withheld any information that may be relevant? (If so, why? Whose interests am I serving by doing so?)

After the Initial Interview:

Have I been clear so far about what I see as the merits and deficiencies in the case the client thinks he has?

Does the client seem open to striving for a win/win solution?
- What might such a solution look like in this case? (Even better, ask the client this.)

Is he willing to take any responsibility for the problem? If he is willing to forgo the role of victim, what opportunities does that open up?
- Can he admit that there were things he could have done that might have prevented the current problem? If so, can he take an active role in resolving it?

Does the client appear to need permission to let go of his anger, and would he accept that permission from me?

How attached is the client to winning? Would anything short of winning be interpreted as success?

What would it mean to me to win this case?

Is the client deluding himself about any aspect of the case?

What might be the best way to start a dialogue?

What ways of looking at this case might locate deeper meanings and broader implications? For example, are there family implications that may at first not be apparent? Community issues? Spiritual issues for the client? How might these implications matter?

Have I made it clear enough that I consider this relationship
- important to me?
- worthy of my time?
- not only a legal but also a human partnership?
- a collaboration in which we each have much to contribute?

With Opposing Counsel:

Am I being honest and forthright?

Am I letting his words or behavior
- get the better of me?
- be an excuse for behaving without integrity?
- make me react unmindfully—that is, reflexively and unconsciously?

Am I taking his words or tactics personally?

Am I behaving with integrity?

If It Goes to Court:

Am I doing all I can to minimize harm to my client?

Am I showing respect for the humanity of the other side, regardless of their brutishness?

Am I striving to help my client maintain the highest degree of consciousness regarding both the legal and the psychological/emotional dimensions of the case?

Am I being sensitive to opportunities to minimize suffering, or to heal?

This list is not meant to be exhaustive, only to suggest that you have many choices to make which, in the aggregate, can reflect deeply held spiritual as well as intellectual and ethical values. This can make your relationships much richer and more fulfilling than you might have thought possible.

"I find that clients are very often looking for a practical reason for doing the right thing," says Michael, a partner with a San Francisco law firm. "In many cases, I hold out options, explaining the positives and negatives of each. I'll show them that there is a mean thing to do and a classy thing to do. I find that people will gravitate toward the classy thing and grab onto how doing something mean will haunt them in the courtroom, either because the judge won't look kindly on it, or because it could hamper settlement."

More often than not, it is the lawyer, not the client, who sets the tone for the relationship. The average client is not particularly sophisticated where the law is concerned, is often overwrought, and wants to feel confident in her lawyer's abilities and commitment to her cause. The form that commitment takes—whether it is to obtaining the least costly, most amicable solution possible or, conversely, to rubbing the opponent's nose in his perceived misdeeds—can make all the difference in the tenor of the entire case.

"Often people will call and ask, 'Can you stand up to my wife's lawyer?' or 'Are you tough enough to handle this?'" says Rita Pollack, a family relations lawyer in Brookline, Massachusetts. "It is possible to transform that situation, but you've got to get them in the door first," she says. "My answer to their question is always, 'Yes, I can do that,' because I know I can. It's the way I used to practice. But my question to them then becomes, 'Is that the best approach? Let's talk about some other things we might do.'"

Seek the Joy in Your Craft

Meaning and pleasure are present when work can be savored.

For Kenji Kanazawa of Honolulu, that realization came rather late. At eighty-two, he is retired and takes on legal work only now and then to keep his mind sharp. "A document that I would have drafted in a morning now takes me quite a while," he says. "I get to enjoy the intricacies of it. I see the different issues, the ramifications. I enjoy thinking about it and the very different ways you can do it. When you're practicing, you choose the best way, and bingo, you finish it up. If you have more time, you can really enjoy it."

For too many lawyers, the pleasure of craft is overlooked. Ronald Kessel, managing partner of Boston's Palmer & Dodge, thinks today's large-firm lawyers are a lot like nineteenth-century New England mill workers. "We have taken the long mill buildings in Lawrence and Lowell, stood them on end, moved them to Boston, and replaced their workers with lawyers. We have become nineteenth-century pieceworkers with harbor rather than river views," he complains.

Kessel is on to something crucial here. When we begin to feel that work is imposed on us, we begin to lose ourselves. Before the advent of the nineteenth-century mills, workers' days were centered around the demands of their craft, dictated not by someone else, but by the worker's own investment of himself, through his hands into the raw material before him. Kessel mourns the passing of a time when lawyers did the same, fretting over details of draftsmanship, for example, that mattered to them even if they would likely be the only ones ever to know the difference.

You can still see the hunger for the pure pleasure of craft on Saturdays, when so many lawyers spend at least part of the day in the office. Some—perhaps most—do it simply because they have to, there being too little time during the week to get everything done. But others go in for a different reason: it's quieter, phones rarely ring, and the work *feels* different in that atmosphere. During the week, time pressures tend to squeeze out what joy may be found in immersing yourself in the peculiarities and nuances of a case, but on Saturdays, time seems somehow to be more forgiving. You can play with your materials, turn things over and consider them from different angles, then go at the work like a carpenter or a sculptor, taking satisfaction in the mysterious interplay of your tools and your talent.

You need to realize that it isn't necessary to retire or to spend all your free time at the office in order to get the Saturday high that many lawyers seek. You can bring it into your weekdays as well. By first using "Time-Out" strategies or brief meditations to clear your mind, for example, you can then sustain your awareness of the moment through mindful breathing, thereby putting yourself *there*, in the office, present and clear, to delight in the subtle shades and textures of lawyering. The "skillful means" technique outlined in Chapter 5 is another way of savoring your craft while still meeting deadlines.

Shift Your Focus

Too many lawyers suffer from what Benjamin Sells calls the "Quit or Cope" syndrome. They are miserable at work, yet they can often think of only two ways to deal with the problem: quit, or cope (that is, talk themselves into believing it's not really so bad).

But that doesn't have to be the case. Trying the practices in this book can help you begin to see alternatives. Mindfulness, contemplation, listening—all these can help you make clear the spectrum of choices available to you, not just in any given moment, but at every point in your life.

Not atypical is the lawyer who was in such great pain that he told his wife he was quitting the law to become a social worker. Panicking, his wife asked Barbara Reinhold, director of career development at Smith College, to meet with him. "He told me he'd been making money by seeing relationships come unglued," Reinhold recalls. "Now, he said, he knew enough about bad relationships that he could help people form good ones, and so he wanted to give up his six-figure salary." As it turned out, his commitments were such that he couldn't just pick up and leave. And it was a good thing, too, because it forced him to look for a way to stay where he was *and* find spiritual nourishment. With Reinhold's help, he decided to switch gears by taking part-time courses in mediation, counseling, and family work. Much to his delight, his colleagues supported him.

Find a Mentor

Finding a mentor is truly an act of will; nobody's going to do it for you. Not these days. Surveys show that well over half of all lawyers lack a mentor who shows interest in their careers. Yet, every lawyer, particularly younger ones, could use such a person, someone whose strength of character and years in practice have enabled him to see through the soul-squashing elements of practice.

In this day and age, with all the pressures that impinge on people in the profession, it may be unrealistic to think you'll find a mentor who can coach you in the development of necessary skills and dispense sage advice on living a life in the law.

Instead, you might try for two mentors—or more. Jon Levy, formerly a sole practitioner and now a judge in York, Maine, says that the best way he found to learn the "hows" of practicing law was to find lawyers you respect and watch them work. That may take the form of going down to the courthouse or, if you're a real estate lawyer, going to closings. It's a way of establishing a relationship with someone whose work you admire.

But there is another, underutilized way to do it: if you occasionally refer cases to other lawyers, either because they're too complicated or because they fall outside of your practice area, refer them to the best law-

 Mentor Meeting Grounds

What can you do if you're looking for a mentor who not only knows the legal ropes but also has an active spiritual life and a sense of how it can be expressed in law practice? If you are a member of a religious community, you might begin by broaching the subject with members of your church, synagogue, mosque, or other institution. Or try contacting the International Alliance of Holistic Lawyers, which can guide you to lawyers in your area who might share your concerns. Contact information can be found in Chapter 10.

yers you can, and *make it known that you come with the case*. This will cost you some, since you get the same referral fee whether or not you tag along with your client, but you'll learn a great deal, from the master of your choosing. For Levy, this approach led to several ongoing relationships with senior lawyers whose friendship and advice proved invaluable.

A More Meaning-full Practice

Transcendent meaning can be found in every life, but only if you are willing to look for it and to recognize in your joys and sorrows, your frustrations and yearnings, opportunities for inner growth. It's an ancient message, common to all the great religious traditions, and it has been the source of hope and a sense of significance for millennia.

Consider these scenarios:

A lawyer begins his day dreading the head-banging that he knows awaits him in a divorce settlement conference. With his first cup of coffee and the morning paper, he begins pulling himself together, gradually steeling himself for battle. "It's a living," he says to himself as he gets in his car.

A second lawyer, facing a similar challenge, sees an opportunity to learn something about herself by doing everything she can to avoid dehumanizing the other side. Failing to do so, she has found, has the effect of flattening her own world, draining away from her work the possibility of fun, surprise, or even, on occasion, the experience of joy. After breakfast, she sits quietly for fifteen minutes, doing nothing but being aware of the importance of keeping an open heart as she begins her workday.

The first lawyer is merely coping. The second has found a spiritual path and a way to express it in her practice. It's a matter of choice. You can choose the lens through which to view your work, keeping in mind that the choices you make as an individual lawyer will have an impact on the larger legal culture. Ideas, actions, and attitudes create ripples that ultimately affect everyone.

The legal profession has begun, in a small way, to open itself to the wholeness imperative that is now very much in evidence in the non-legal world. To do so on a wider level may be the ticket to hastening the journey to a new, more satisfying professional reality. As a society—one in which lawyers play a key and potentially transformative role—we are starting to realize that pain really is part of the human condition, and that we can't buy, work, or fight our way into a trouble-free existence. That being so, maybe it's time to determine the *why* of your predicament, why you—with your unique history, gifts, strengths, and weaknesses— are where you are now, where you want your story to go from here, and how your legal career can be part of a move in the right direction.

The bottom line is this: you can have an awakened inner life, one that can nourish your professional life so that what you *do* becomes more of an expression of who you *are*. It can be a kind of homecoming, a return to a place that feels familiar yet utterly new. It can bring excitement back to your law practice.

Transforming Your Practice

There isn't a lawyer in practice who hasn't had to work hard to get where she is today. Focused, determined effort is part of the path. But many lawyers' capacity for applying themselves to a problem and working hard to solve it deserts them when the problem is their own unhappiness. Maybe it's because that problem is more amorphous than the ones on the bar exam, or the one facing you when you set out to build a career with all the trappings of success. For that, the road is pretty well marked.

The road to happiness in law practice is not so clear. But that's because lawyers tend to see it as separate from the rest of their lives, so that the resources available for gaining some kind of inner peace appear to have little relevance in the office. Once you see through that delusion and come to realize that your own sense of what really matters in life is *totally* relevant in your practice, you will have the handle you need. You can then begin to make choices that will bring you satisfaction, perhaps even joy.

A few choices that might help:

- Find a colleague with whom you can discuss ways to renew your love of practicing law. Don't let the idea that "It just isn't done" stop you from trying. The fellowship will be incredibly rewarding.
- Make a list of three things you feel helpless to change. Then figure out how to change them.
- Take a senior member of the firm to dinner, and invite his advice and wisdom.

If you're a young associate at a law firm, you actually have more room to move than you might think. There are choices you can make that are personally enriching and mitigate against the stifling qualities of law firm life.

- Choose to be conscious, aware, present. That way, you open up the opportunities before you and realize the various junctures at which you can choose to be caring, compassionate, even loving.
- Choose to understand and work through your own tendencies to become aggressive or angry. Understanding yourself at this level helps free you from reflexive negativity.
- Show that you care about your colleagues *as people*. They will notice your interest, and eventually, they will start talking to you about themselves.
- Cultivate friendships with people who appear willing to talk about how they really feel about law and the way it's practiced.
- Take time at least once a day to think about the things you feel grateful for.

CHAPTER FOURTEEN

TRANSITION AND OPPORTUNITY

Meaning or purpose serves as a point of reference.
As long as we keep purpose in focus in both our
organizational and personal lives, we are able to
wander through the realms of chaos, and emerge
with a discernible pattern or shape to our lives.

—*Margaret Wheatley*
Leadership and the New Science

IT IS A POPULAR PASTIME AMONG lawyers these days to wonder, both to themselves and aloud, who will be left standing after the millennial changes that seem certain to transform the profession come about.

No one knows the answer for sure, but one thing seems ever more likely: lawyers who distinguish themselves by virtue of their own wholeness, as it is expressed in their generous humanity and sensitivity to clients' need for meaning, will thrive. Others are likely to founder.

There are several reasons for this. First, it is axiomatic that the stronger and healthier you are emotionally, spiritually, and physically, the better able you'll be to thrive in a world where certainty is illusory and the rules are fluid. The relationship between the modern world and mental well-being is clear: you cannot cope with a chaotic and unpredictable living and working environment without having a very strong sense of place and footing.

The lawyer who thrives will be the one who is nimble enough to play a variety of roles for his clients and is sufficiently centered to ride successive waves of change without losing a sense of equilibrium. Jim Champy, coauthor of the influential business book *Re-Engineering the Corporation*, says that in the business context, lawyers will have to be sensitive to a whole range of profound human issues. "There is deep stuff afoot in business," he says. "It's pushing management into some fundamental questions," concerning the very nature of business and its place in the contemporary world. "They are having to make decisions without highly tuned sensibilities, and they're struggling. People are searching for answers to basic questions, many of which have to do with what organizations' core values are. And when you're in that deep transitional space, people will tend to fall back on the spiritual."

Lawyers, says Champy, should be involved in this momentous discussion. They should be there where the great questions of identity and relevance are being hashed out. "The value-added of the practice of law is not in the preparation of documents—which will be commoditized—it will be in the deep debates around the nature of business," says Champy. "Good counsel will have to be attentive to that sort of thing."

The kind of attention Champy is describing cannot be faked. It's easy enough to become conversant in an industry's concerns and peculiarities, but that kind of knowledge is fungible—it's all outer-world stuff. When Champy talks about *fundamental* questions, he means the kind that aren't answered in legal texts; they require personal, human answers, from the lawyer's heart, soul, and mind to the client's. To provide that, a lawyer must be grounded in his own reality, open to alternative realities, and conversant in the language of the heart as well as the law. His job will then be to help facilitate deeper awareness of the meanings that matter most to the client.

One theme of this book that has not been overtly stated but is frequently implied is that spiritual practice makes the invisible visible. Through conscious attention to the inner as well as the outer life, we become aware of things we used to miss. The connective tissue of society, for example—not only economic and political, but also emotional and spiritual—becomes ever clearer. Seeing these connections, the lawyer can factor in the human meanings that underlie legal entanglements, using this new resource to fashion more fitting solutions for clients who need more than just legal advice.

As Champy suggested in his comment on how some of lawyers' current functions will become commoditized, technology's impact on law practice is likely to be increasingly jarring. It isn't hard to envision a scenario in which a client in need of a particular document—even something rather complicated—logs on to the Internet and tracks one down. He might even find a winning brief on an issue very close to the one that concerns him. He'll point and click, contact the author of the brief, and arrange to have similar work done for him. Less complicated work will he cheap and easy to find. It's inevitable, and when it happens, lawyers will sink or swim depending on what they can bring to a client that the client can't find with a mouse—in a word, wisdom.

Criminal defense lawyer Sam Guiberson has given this a lot of thought. "Look around you," he says. "How much of what you do is becoming available in the enriched information and communications environment we live in? If what you sell becomes a devalued coin, you can't trade in products; you have to trade in essences. No guild can survive when its craft is ubiquitous. The only one that will survive is one that has a sense of the value of values, the value of essences."

BEGINNING THE DISCUSSION

It is time to start talking, time to end the self-imposed gag rules that prevent lawyers from discussing what really matters to them, how they really feel about law practice, and what they dream the practice might become. Conversation, when entered into with a spirit of openness, is another means of making the invisible visible. When problems are named, they lose some of their bite and can be viewed realistically; when feelings and perceptions come to the fore, they often reveal a strong commonality among those involved in the discussion; when memories of moments when law practice gave much more than it asked for are shared, the yearning for a better way begins to coalesce; and when misgivings about the direction the profession has taken are aired, the desire for change can be harnessed. There is a great deal of locked-up emotion in the profession. Denying it does no one any good. It's time to face—on a profession-wide level—what is really going on in the lives of lawyers.

Individual lawyers must begin testing the waters of self-disclosure. It has to start somewhere. On the institutional level too, methods for facilitating open and honest dialogue will be essential. The Northeastern University Law School professional development program described in Chapter 12 holds great promise for getting past such outer distractions as titles and hierarchies to the beating heart of the profession. So does the contemplative approach used by the Green Group and discussed in Chapter 4.

One technique being used by innovative organizations all over the world to generate new ideas is called simply "Dialogue." Developed by the late David Bohm, a Nobel Prize–winning physicist who saw the creation of meaning as essentially an interpersonal activity, Dialogue—from the root *dialogos*, or "flow of meaning"—may be an ideal antidote for the close-to-the-vest secretiveness that the legal culture encourages. The name alone suggests how different it is from processes more commonly used in the legal context: "debate"—which actually means "to beat down"—and "discussion"—which shares its root with "percussion" and "concussion" and means "to break things up."

A metaphor helps to clarify what is involved in the process of Dialogue: just as water has a natural tendency to flow toward the sea, Bohm contended, meaning naturally flows toward coherence. Like water, meaning too can be blocked in its natural movement if it encounters obstacles in its path. Dialogue is a process for dealing with such obstacles, so that the flow of meaning can continue unimpeded.

The process has something in common with meditation, in that it allows—on the group level—for the observation of thought while it is occurring, thus revealing the subtleties that control group interactions. In Dialogue, no idea, thought, feeling, or observation is ever treated as inferior to or better than any other. This nonjudgmental, free-flowing process is one way of bringing each participant's inner life—in the form of feelings, intuitions, and creativity—into contact with others'.

What happens when Dialogue is working, according to people who have experienced it, is that it makes possible an understanding of the kinds of processes that interfere with real communication between individuals, as well as different parts of the same organization. It allows for a kind of exchange that emphasizes the *being* side of the being/doing dichotomy.

If the legal profession as it now exists is a reflection of the ways lawyers think, it won't be possible to change the profession without changing its characteristic thought patterns. By shining a light on the moment-to-moment reality of those processes, Dialogue—rather like mindfulness—is yet another way of making the invisible visible and thereby expanding awareness. Such a technique would be new to the legal world, and time must be put aside to explore its potential.

MODELS FOR EXPLORATION

Since 1990, the Nathan Cummings Foundation in New York City has sponsored programs in the fields of health, the arts, and the environment that all have one thing in common: integrating spirituality into the search for solutions to the pervasive problems facing society. Having become aware of a spiritual reawakening in the world today, the Foundation created these programs in response to what it perceived as a yearning for new sources of answers, new vehicles for solving problems, and new ways to find meaning in our individual and collective lives.

The legal profession could use such a program. Having looked outward, into the world of action, analysis, and codification, and all but exhausted the possibilities there, it is now time to find the courage to look inward for insight and new sources of inspiration. The need is simply too great to be ignored. Such a program might explore any number of issues, including:

- how to close the gap between lawyers' personal values and the work they do
- how to understand what it means to be a "whole" lawyer and to support it as a goal for all practitioners
- how to make personal growth an integral part of professional development
- how cultivating the inner life can help lawyers take back control of their lives in the face of billable-hour pressures and client demands
- how developing the inner life of law firms can strengthen the glue that holds them together

A final tool for making the invisible visible comes from Joel Barker, an author, teacher, and consultant to corporations, who regularly asks his clients what he calls the "what if" question: *What* is the one thing that you cannot do in your industry that, *if* it could be done, would fundamentally change things for the better?

Some have already applied this question to the legal profession. At an ABA conference on the future of law practice, two of the more popular proposals were deregulating the practice so that lawyers and nonlawyers could form partnerships, and abolishing hourly billing. Neither appears to be imminent, but clearly both would have significant impact.

Here's another answer worth considering: *Begin a conversation on the role of the inner life—of spirituality, if you will—in law practice.* Bring the discussion into law firms, to bar association functions, and into informal chats among lawyers, making it real, relevant, and practical. Much that is now invisible would become clear: resistance and skepticism, to be sure, but also a sense of longing and a profound relief. It would take courage, and perhaps an initial willingness to suspend disbelief. But stranger things have happened. The Berlin Wall came down, and Nelson Mandela was elected president of South Africa.

These comparisons may sound outlandish, but are they? To most people—perhaps even to most lawyers—such a profession-wide discussion must appear as far-fetched as the events in Germany and South Africa seemed only a short time before they happened. But the energy released by those events—and the new possibilities they unleashed—are worth considering in the context of the proposed discussion in the legal world. The rewards could be enormous, beginning with a reimagining of what lawyering can be and what professionalism is all about.

These tools, these ways of making the invisible come into focus, offer great promise for lawyers, who have a unique role in working with what Fetzer Institute president Rob Lehman refers to as the "tissue of the outer life"—that is, the law itself. Bringing an awareness of subsurface realities into the mix will take patience, courage, and determination. Patience, because a culture cannot be changed in a day. Courage, because it takes guts to try something new, to refuse to sell yourself or your profession short, and to go beyond seeing everything in terms of winning and losing. And determination—a trait shared by all good lawyers—because the forces of complacency are tenacious.

But think about the possible rewards: a new paradigm for success, one that takes into consideration the profession's roots in healing; a renewed respect for the beauty and mystery of what it means to practice law; a new sense of time, one that does not equate it with dollars and cents; and a new appreciation for the role of intuition, particularly as it relates to what clients seek from their lawyers. These are tools for living an authentic life into the next century, for integrating work and meaning, for bringing to the law ways of knowing and being that have for too long been dismissed as irrelevant.

LIGHT ON THE HORIZON

How do people become awake and open to deeper levels of their own inner life and being?

This question, first presented in Chapter 1, seems an apt place to end. Becoming open and awake is what this moment and future moments demand of lawyers if the legal profession is to once again bring real satisfaction to its members and comfort and sustenance to the public.

There is no greater gift than awareness. Nothing in life—not beauty, not love, not even the concept of value itself—is of any value without it. And yet, in the modern world, we tend to sell it so cheaply, giving it up to the noise and the rush of each too-busy moment. But as a lawyer you can make a great difference—greater than you might imagine—in your own life and in the lives of others, by reclaiming your right to a balanced awareness of both the inner and outer dimensions of life. You have the tools to cultivate that awareness, practices that provide a direct experience of what it means to become more present to who you are and what you need, to awaken those deeper levels of your own inner life and being.

So look first to yourself. Then look to each other. Start talking. If you need an opening, or an excuse, to broach these issues, use this book. Mention it and the ideas it touches on.

"There comes a time when you find that you've promised yourself to things that are just too small," the poet David Whyte has said. If his words resonate with you, let the feelings they evoke guide you. And allow yourself the luxury of having some faith that, although the light may as yet be dim, the growing power of your awareness—especially when united with that of your professional colleagues—will concentrate and enhance it so that it may yet show the way to something larger.

BIBLIOGRAPHY
AND RECOMMENDED
READINGS

Bachman, Walt. *Law v. Life: What Lawyers Are Afraid to Say About the Legal Profession*. Rhinebeck, NY: Four Directions Press, 1995.

Bass, Ellen. *The Courage to Heal*. New York: HarperPerennial, 1994.

Bellow, Gary, and Martha Minow, eds. *Law Stories: Law, Meaning and Violence*. Ann Arbor: University of Michigan Press, 1998.

Bennett, Merit. *Law and the Heart: A Practical Guide for Successful Lawyer/Client Relationships*. Santa Fe: The Message Company, 1996.

Bowles, Paul Frederick. *The Sunday Times* (London) Books section. July 23, 1989.

Briskin, Alan. *The Stirring of Soul in the Workplace*. San Francisco: Berrett-Kohler Publishers, 1996.

Brussat, Frederic, and Mary Ann Brussat. *Spiritual Literacy: Reading the Sacred in Everyday Life*. New York: Scribner, 1996.

Bush, Robert Baruch, and Joseph P. Folger. *The Promise of Mediation: Responding to Conflict Through Empowerment and Recognition*. San Francisco: Jossey-Bass, 1994.

Carter, Terry. "Rankled by the Rankings." *ABA Journal* 84 (Mar. 1998): 46.

Chittester, Joan. *There Is a Season*. Maryknoll, NY: Orbis Books, 1995.

Cooper, David. *Simplicity and Solitude: A Guide for Spiritual Retreat*. New York: Bell Tower, 1992.

Csikszentmihalyi, Mihaly. *Finding Flow: The Psychology of Engagement with Everyday Life*. New York: Basic Books, 1997.

——. *Flow: The Psychology of Optimal Experience*. New York: Harper-Collins, 1990.

Dass, Ram, and Mirabai Bush. *Compassion in Action: Setting Out on the Path of Service*. New York: Crown Publishers, 1995.

Dossey, Larry. *Healing Words: The Power of Prayer and the Practice of Medicine*. New York: HarperCollins, 1993.

——. *Prayer is Good Medicine: How to Reap the Healing Benefits of Prayer*. New York: HarperCollins, 1996.

Eliot, T. S. "Little Gidding" from *Four Quartets*. New York: Harcourt Brace & Company, 1943, 1971.

Ellinor, Linda, and Glenna Gerard. *Dialogue: Rediscover the Transforming Power of Conversation*. New York: John Wiley & Sons, Inc., 1998.

Elliott, James A. "Lawyers Helping Lawyers: 25." *Georgia State Bar Review* 25, no. 3 (Feb. 1989).

Fowler, George. *Learning to Dance Inside: Getting to the Heart of Meditation*. New York: Addison-Wesley, 1996.

Fox, Matthew. *The Reinvention of Work*. San Francisco: Harper-SanFrancisco, 1994.

Frankl, Victor. *Man's Search for Meaning*. New York: Washington Square Press, 1998.

Gandhi, Mohandas K. *An Autobiography: The Story of My Experiments with Truth*. Boston: Beacon Press, 1993.

Gatland, Laura. "Dangerous Dedication." *ABA Journal* 83 (Dec. 1997): 28.

Glendon, Mary Ann. *A Nation Under Lawyers: How the Crisis in the Legal Profession Is Transforming American Society*. Cambridge, MA: Harvard University Press, 1994.

Goldstein, Joseph. *Insight Meditation: The Practice of Freedom.* Boston: Shambhala, 1993.

Goleman, Daniel. *Vital Lies, Simple Truths: The Psychology of Self-Deception.* New York: Simon & Schuster, 1995.

Hanh, Thich Nhat. *The Miracle of Mindfulness.* Boston: Beacon Press, 1975.

Heschel, Abraham Joshua. *God in Search of Man: A Philosophy of Judaism.* New York: Noonday Press, 1997.

"The Impact of Impaired Attorneys on the Texas Grievance Process." *Texas Bar Journal* 52, no. 3 (Mar. 1989): 312–14.

Jacobius, Arlene. "Coming Back from Depression." *ABA Journal* 82 (April 1996): 74.

Jaworski, Joseph. *Synchronicity: The Inner Path of Leadership.* San Francisco: Berrett-Kohler, 1996.

Kabat-Zinn, Jon. *Everyday Blessings: The Inner Work of Mindful Parenting.* New York: Hyperion, 1997.

———. *Wherever You Go, There You Are: Mindfulness Meditation in Everyday Life.* New York: Hyperion, 1994.

———. *Full Catastrophe Living: Using the Wisdom of Your Body and Mind to Face Stress, Pain and Illness.* New York: Delta, 1990.

Kane, William John, and Cheryl Baisden. "Use and Abuse: Are You Controlling the Substance, or Is the Substance Controlling You?" *New Jersey Lawyer* 181 (Dec. 1996): 12.

Kaufman, George W. *The Lawyer's Guide to Balancing Life and Work: Taking the Stress Out of Success.* Chicago: American Bar Association Law Practice Management Section, 1999.

Keen, Sam. *Fire in the Belly: On Being a Man.* New York: Bantam Doubleday Dell Publishers, 1992.

Kessel, Ronald H. "On Matters of the Spirit." *Boston Bar Journal* 36, no. 5 (Nov./Dec. 1992).

Kornfield, Jack. *A Path with Heart: A Guide Through the Perils and Promises of Spiritual Life.* New York: Bantam Books, 1993.

Kundtz, David. *Stopping: How to Be Still When You Have to Keep Going.* Berkeley, CA: Conari Press, 1998.

Leider, Richard. "Are You Deciding on Purpose?" *Fast Company* (Feb./Mar. 1998): 114.

Levine, Stephen. *A Year to Live: How to Live This Year As If It Were Your Last*. New York: Bell Tower, 1997.

Levoy, Gregg. *Callings: Finding and Following an Authentic Life*. New York: Three Rivers Press, 1998.

Lynch, James J. *The Broken Heart*. New York: Basic Books, 1977; Baltimore: Bancroft Press, 1998.

———. *The Language of the Heart*. New York: Basic Books, 1985; Baltimore: Bancroft Press, 1998.

MacLeish, Archibald. "Apologia." *The Harvard Law Review* 85, no. 8 (June 1972).

Maisel, Eric. *Fearless Creativity: A Step-by-Step Guide to Starting and Completing Your Work of Art*. New York: Putnam, 1995.

McQuiston, John II. *Always We Begin Again: The Benedictine Way of Living*. Ridgefield, CT: Morehouse Publishing, 1996.

Moyers, Bill. *Healing and the Mind*. New York: Doubleday, 1993.

Muller, Wayne. *Legacy of the Heart: The Spiritual Advantages of a Painful Childhood*. New York: Fireside, 1995.

"The 9 Best Ways to De-Stress: The Nature Connection." At www.homearts.com/gh/health/09stbub.htm. The Hearst Corporation, 1995.

O'Donahue, John. *Eternal Echoes: Exploring Our Yearning to Belong*. New York: HarperCollins, 1999.

Ornish, Dean. *Love and Survival: The Scientific Basis for the Healing Power of Intimacy*. New York: HarperCollins, 1998.

Pearsall, Paul. *The Pleasure Prescription: To Love, to Work, to Play—Life in the Balance*. Alameda, CA: Hunter House, 1996.

Pennehaker, James W. *Opening Up: The Healing Power of Confiding in Others*. New York: William Morrow & Company, 1990.

Powell, Thomas Reed. Quoted in *The Symbols of Government* (page 120) by Thurman W. Arnold. New Haven: Yale University Press, 1935.

Ray, Paul H. *The Integral Culture Survey: A Study of the Emergence of Transformational Values in America*. Sausalito, CA: The Institute of Noetic Sciences, 1996.

Rechtschaffen, Stephan. *Timeshifting: Creating More Time to Enjoy Your Life*. New York: Doubleday, 1996.

Remen, Rachel Naomi. *Kitchen Table Wisdom: Stories That Heal*. New York: Riverhead Books, 1996.

Rilke, Rainer Maria. *Selected Poems of Rainer Maria Rilke*. Translation and Commentary by Robert Bly. New York: Harper and Row, 1981.

Schulweis, Harold. Rosh Hashanah sermon, 1996. Valley Beth Shalom Synagogue, Encino, California.

Sells, Benjamin. *The Soul of the Law: Understanding Lawyers and the Law*. Rockport, MA: Element, 1994.

Simms, George. *Keeping Your Personal Journal*. Mahwah, NJ: Paulist Press, 1978.

The State of the Legal Profession. Chicago: American Bar Association, Young Lawyers Division, 1991.

Steindl-Rast, David, and Sharon Lebell. *The Music of Silence*. New York: HarperCollins, 1995.

Sullivan, Paula Farrell. *The Mystery of My Story: Autobiographical Writing for Personal and Spiritual Development*. Mahwah, NJ: Paulist Press, 1991.

Tarlton, Merrilyn Astin. "On Being Human." *Law Practice Management* 22, no. 5 (July/Aug. 1996): 25.

Tart, Charles T. *Living the Mindful Life: A Handbook for Living in the Present Moment*. Boston: Shambhala, 1994.

Task Force on Professional Fulfillment. *Expectations, Reality and Recommendations for Change: The Report of the Boston Bar Association*. Boston: Boston Bar Association, 1997.

Tulku, Tarthang. *Skillful Means: Patterns for Success*. Berkeley, CA: Dharma Publishing, 1991.

Wheatley, Margaret. *Leadership and the New Science: Learning About Organization from an Orderly Universe*. San Francisco: Berrett-Kohler Publishers, 1994.

Whyte, David. *The Heart Aroused: Poetry and the Preservation of the Soul in Corporate America*. New York: Currency Doubleday, 1994.

Wilber, Ken. *Grace and Grit: Spirituality and Healing in the Life and Death of Treya Killam Wilber*. Boston: Shambhala, 1993.

202 | TRANSFORMING PRACTICES

———. *A Brief History of Everything.* Boston: Shambhala, 1996.

Zaleski, Philip, and Paul Kaufman. *Gifts of the Spirit: Living the Wisdom of the Great Religious Traditions.* San Francisco: Harper-SanFrancisco, 1997.

INDEX

ABOUT THE
AUTHOR

STEVEN KEEVA IS a former assistant managing editor of the *ABA Journal*. The winner of numerous awards for his feature writing, he has a graduate degree from Northwestern University's Medill School of Journalism, at which he has also taught legal affairs reporting.

Steven has written on a range of topics—including the law, parenting and family issues—for magazines in the United States, Australia, Great Britain, and Japan. His articles for the *ABA Journal* have been used as instructional materials by bar associations nationwide and by numerous educational institutions, including Harvard University, New York University School of Law, Northwestern University School of Law, U.C. Berkeley, and the Catholic University School of Law. He speaks nationally about finding deeper meaning and greater satisfaction in professional life.

Steven encourages readers to send comments, questions, and especially stories to TransformingPractices@yahoo.com.